Blanche H. Clemmer

THE CONTRAST

THE
CONTRAST

BY

**HILAIRE
BELLOC**

NEW YORK
ROBERT M. McBRIDE & COMPANY
MCMXXIV

To
Mr. and Mrs. Hoffman Nickerson,
My hosts in New York.

Kingsland,
November 2nd, 1923.

CONTENTS

THE CONTRAST

I

THE SURPRISE

WHEN I first crossed the ocean to the New World it was in an adventure of boyhood: I was not yet of age; Discovery tempted me and the hunger for new things. Had I known indeed what a transition I was attempting, what a border I was crossing, the immeasurable disparities before me, my adventure would have seemed far greater; I should have been drawn to it more intensely, but should have feared it more.

I went as every man goes, who starts from Europe upon that western quest; I went with no conception of the revolution awaiting my mind.

After I had journeyed on the ocean many days in no great comfort, for I did not travel as the rich travel, I came to a part of the sea where all things changed.

It was in crossing the Grand Banks that I discovered this new air; I was appalled and vastly intrigued. I was coming to unknown things. It was in what I breathed and in the quality of the wind.

The ancients had a phrase, "new stars." They said of the exile or the wanderer, "He came to know new stars . . ." and that phrase has puzzled many. For the adventurer of the old Mediterranean went eastward and westward and saw no new stars. What did our Roman fathers mean by that phrase? Those wise men meant "New Influences," using the word "stars" for that mysterious thing, the influence of heaven.

Here I know that I run a great risk at the outset of this book. When I say that I as a boy thus came to "New Stars," and was in a strange air from the hour in which the boat lay under undiscovered land, I shall not at first be received by my contemporaries, but shall seem to be talking nonsense. It is the fate of all who tell a truth worth telling, especially when they tell it for what is perhaps the first time. Anyhow, this book is personal, and if the testimony it gives sound at first eccentric or absurd, let it stand and do its work for what it is: the true testimony of one mind. The heavens did have new influence before the sea was crossed, and I did already perceive by every sense known and unknown that I was upon the threshold of new things.

How rapidly, how sharply, did that impression grow!

The first light-ship twinkling upon the horizon was like a herald. I wondered at the coming world; and when I passed through the Narrows into New York Harbour, I saw grass and trees, contours of low hills, the houses of men, and all was utterly strange.

I landed. The first phrase of popular speech I heard was incomprehensible, the more incomprehensible because I expected it to be in my own idiom; much the more incomprehensible because it was incomprehensible through a manner and spirit of diction more than through verbal form. The new speech rapidly grew familiar to me; in a day or two I could make myself understood with repetitions and talking slowly, while, with great care, I could understand at the first saying most of what was said to me in the streets. But the impression of strangeness was the more accentuated by that experience of learning. It was astonishing that, with what I had always thought to be our own English language, such a process should be necessary!

With every succeeding experience accumulated in day after day of multitudinous travel, this truth—that I had come (in the fullest sense of that word "world") into an unknown *world,* grew within me. I crossed the great plains, I

lingered in the mountains. I had granted to me
the miracle and vision of California. I looked at
last upon the Pacific.

I was free in those days; and during the
months that followed I took my way as I would:
very often for whole weeks on foot, sometimes
riding or driving, here and there, then cutting
out great spaces through the railway, and then
on foot again for weeks in the lonely places
of the west. I handled the salt dust of the
deserts and I watched the faces and the gestures
of these new men, these foreigners. I drew the
mountains in sepia for my pleasure and their
snows. And, by the way, having lost my very
small stock of money at cards (playing against
more cunning and older men in a deep valley
of the hills) I cheerfully procured my further
progress by the selling of these pictures to mountain men. I would make a good little sketch in
sepia of some peak, and this a lonely fellow on
a ranch was very glad to have, giving me in exchange my supper, my breakfast and my bed;
and I would go on next day to another, and
draw another picture and sell it for another
lodging. Then, when I got to the plains again,
I went back quickly day and night eastward. I
stayed with friends once more on the Atlantic
seaboard, and I returned to my own place.

*   *   *   *   *

There had been added to me an experience
which has left me for the rest of my life determined that no one knows a human thing who
has not seen and handled it. In this particular
thing of America I had learnt, as fully as one
learns a conviction of one's own mind, as fully
as one knows one's own mood, that it was, with
every adjective and adverb I could use, *alien,
foreign, different:* not Europe, not Africa not
the Old World at all. In each smallest differ-
ential of a million details The Contrast was apparent. In the integration of the whole that
Contrast was overwhelming.

I say "with every adjective and adverb one
can use." I shall use many such, even in this
book, and I shall have to repeat them over and
over again: "inexpressible," "incredible," "funda-
mentally," "radically," "profoundly," and so
forth. They are violent yet inadequate—and
words more moderate would be untrue.

Words are here more feeble than in any other
form of their use. For the use of words connotes
a universal similarity between the things to which
they attach. And how shall words be used to
express an essential difference in the very core
of things?

A metaphor may help. You give the name
of a thing, say a table. You talk to any man
of a table and he thinks of the object as he has

known it and of the material *wood*. But supposing that table which is in your mind is not his sort of table at all, not a table of wood but a table of *glass*—How then? Have you told him what you saw? You have not. The whole meaning of the thing is different in your mind from what it is in his, because you are speaking of glass when he thought you were speaking of wood. If he knows glass you can laboriously explain and in part eliminate his error; though probably he will not believe you, even so. But if he does not know glass, what are you to do? You can only by further parallels and qualities drawn from quite other things give him an impression most imperfect. He may know transparent things like water, brittle things like pottery. And you may tell him that the material of which you speak is transparent like water and yet brittle like pottery. It will be very difficult for him to combine the two ideas. And as you add to your description of the qualities of glass your task gets more and more difficult, for you disturb more and more his association of ideas: the more truth you tell him, the less easily will he receive it.

Now so it is, and very much more truly then of any simple dead material, when you are speaking of human things. The human experience is almost incommunicable to one that has not had it, and therefore this human experience, the separateness of America, is almost incommunicable. The revolution in sensation which the New World makes upon the European, when, from a happy accident of youth, eager sense, or ignorance and freedom from literary warping he gets it fully and immediately, is almost incommunicable.

How would you communicate the sea to a man who had no experience of the sea? Is it adequate to tell him that the sea is a mass of water stretching out much further than his vision can extend? Certainly not. If you tell him that it is salt, does that communicate the tang and summons of a sea wind? Will he not call up at once in his mind a land-wind—which is of another family? I think he will never know the sea at all unless he sails upon it. And so with the knowledge of that completely New World beyond the immensity of the Atlantic.

*   *   *   *   *

The difficulty of presenting The Contrast is enhanced by two modern conditions which militate heavily against the propagation of all truth in our day. The now universal habit of rapid reading: the formation of the mind in youth by the dead insistent dogmatic assertion of innumerable things unknown to the teacher: not experienced by the teacher. Print and the me-

chanical education of our time are to blame for
these two obstacles to truth.

Both are recent and account between them
for half our follies. Print we have had with
us for more than four hundred years, but its use
for universal, superficial and very hasty reading
is of yesterday: a mechanical education, stand-
ardised, devitalised, hermetically sealed and
sterile is a very recent thing. Neither will last
long, but each will do much more harm before
it crumbles into the dust out of which it was made.
The disease of rapid, universal reading affects
the leisured and the few less than it does the
masses; but in some measure it affects all. The
mechanical, sterilised education is an evil imposed upon the masses by law, which the more
leisured, that is the more rich, largely escape
from; as indeed they escape from most laws.
They can continue for *their* children in some degree the old, liberal and vital manner of teaching.
They can early give them Greek and irony. But
even men thus brought up, as I was, do not escape the bad influence of our time, or its fixed,
certain and self-satisfied ignorance.

This sterilised education, aided by and repos-
ing upon print abused, gives children words
where they should have things, and things where
they should have words. For the severe element
of mathematics it substitutes metaphors; for a

string of dates, which should be the basis of
history, it substitutes ridiculous pictures, giving
Alfred of England the face of a modern Baptist.
But where things are essential and words mis-
leading, as for instance in the telling of what
contemporary and foreign nations are, it gives
the infant dead words instead of living things.
And the Babe, the poor innocent, having had
given him 40 as the number of France and 60
as the number of an exactly parallel label called
"Germany," may go through life to a miserable
old age believing that there really is a certain
simple homogeneous unit called "Germany,"
alike everywhere within its boundaries, and another equally simple homogeneous unit called
France: the two standing side by side, but the
one six and the other four. Now six is greater
than four, and that comparison breeds its own
set of simple falsehoods.

This child becoming a boy, and the boy a lad,
and the lad a man, perhaps a politician, will act
as though this nonsense were sense, and will be
hugely disturbed when the four upon occasion
exceed the six in power. His disappointment
and his trouble of mind will pursue him in this
matter from blunder to blunder until he sinks
into an unhappy grave.

Like all modern men, I had not escaped the
effluvium of this modern disease where America

was concerned. I had read in print of the
Americans, and what I had been told was superficial though prodigiously extended. Therefore
it was untrue in its effects. Had I never read
what Americans had written of themselves nor
any description of what Europeans had reported
upon their return, the shock of the real discovery
would have been less overwhelming. Had anyone given me so much as a hint of the intense
quality of difference between what I had known
and what I was to know, it would have at least
prepared me negatively. But like all my fellows
of the older world I had neither of these advantages. I was not free from some knowledge of
what Americans had written and of how they
presented the air of their own people. For in
Europe all men have some measure of such communication with America, direct or indirect. I
had had much more than most. I had near relatives, American born, a grandmother from
Pennsylvania, and cousins in that State. I met
closely, even so young, a dozen men and women,
not relatives, who had come from the new world
and spoken of it to me perpetually. I had even
been brought up upon what is known to the
older generation of Americans as the "Rollo
Books." And well do I remember my visualisa-
tion, when I was a boy, of the English words
therein which called up in my mind pictures of

English things: pictures of English rivers, English woods, English roads. Pictures as far removed from the reality as it is possible for one thing to be from another. I had received, more than most, the first sort of attack by the spoken and written word denaturalised as it passed from its original source to us. I had also received the second sort of attack (which should be more informing), the attack through those Europeans who had gone to America and returned. Many of my elders spoke to me of the place, having visited it: and I heard what they had to say.

Had I not received any such early communications, had I come as ignorant of the names as I was of the things I was to know, I should perhaps have received a truer immediate impression. It is remarkable that, with regard to alien things, their description through the medium of other minds, native or foreign, blurs reality.

I had then already read much of things written on America and by Americans, and not a few things written by Englishmen and one book written by a learned Frenchman, of whom his enemies said that "he had the defect of looking as though he had known from all eternity that which he had just looked up in an encyclopedia." I heartily wish I had had none of those books which had given me a false conception of the complete, the bewildering novelty I was to find in my transition into this universe of life overwhelmingly removed from my own. All that information was the opposite of truly informing, for it was received through a false psychology.

It would seem as though nothing else can give you what is given you by the eye.

*   *   *   *   *

I am sometimes tempted to declare that discovery is incommunicable.

*   *   *   *   *

But is it incommunicable? Not if the mind of the teller bends itself to the heavy task of translation. With a sufficient sincerity and labour the simple, perhaps, and at any rate direct testimony of the senses, actual vision and hearing and touch and smell, can be conveyed. These things communicate reality to the living witness. Even a modern boy coming to the New World while he is still alive and his senses active discovers the new thing—And so did I. Perhaps, after so many years, I can recover, restore, and present to others the effect of reality.

*   *   *   *   *

After that first, early, vivid lesson I returned, still young, to America. I married there; I came back again and yet again and a fourth time before my thirtieth birthday. I travelled everywhere and spoke to men of every kind.

Twenty-five years passed—the better part of a man's life—and, once more, I returned.

In this last brief glimpse I discovered beneath all the superficial growth and change the same profound, underlying spirit; the same Personality—the soul of which is not ours.

My business is to call up, so late, that early, that now confirmed impression of *Contrast;* to repeat it over and over again and to attempt its analysis. The attempt will be most imperfect, for the vast thing cannot be adequately analysed, only most tentatively so; but I will make the attempt.

*   *   *   *   *

My thesis is that the New World is wholly alien to the Old. Had time proceeded further, were the language become admittedly foreign, the architecture transformed to a new native type, the institutions grown grotesquely diverse between America and Europe (as they will later be), the thesis would be of a different kind and differently approached, above all much easier to advance. The difficulty of presenting it today lies in the existing superficial similarities, and the remaining lessening bonds which mask the essential truth.

Yet the presentation of that essential truth,

however inadequately done and against whatever difficulties of appreciation for the reader, at the risk of whatever ridicule, must be attempted for a very practical reason; which is that, in proportion as this truth of the Contrast is missed, the interaction, especially the political interaction, of the New World with the Old, and more particularly of the New World with the *English* part of the Old, will lead to disasters.

It is the very definition of blunder, that blunder is the uninformed association of disassociated things. It is a blunder to try to keep wine sweet in its jar by putting a square stopper into a round mouth. A man has, let us say, known all his life nothing but the square Dutch stopper of the square-mouthed Dutch pitcher. Hearing that a stopper is needed be brings his square stopper as a matter of course. He blunders. His blunder lies in the conception that the stopper will stop because it is called a stopper: in the association of *all* stoppers with squareness and the corresponding false association of all jars with squareness. The square stopper will not fit the round hole.

It is a blunder to gauge the happiness of human life by the measure of money. The blunder is due to the association of the idea of regular and arithmetical accumulation, which is in the nature of money, with a corresponding regular and arithmetical accumulation of happiness, which is not in the nature of happiness. And this false association proceeds from the false conception that because there is a measure of happiness to be added to by a measure of money in any one case, therefore the process of happiness is, like the process of money, indefinitely prolonged.

Such is blunder; and blunder in political relations is of the same origin: the false association of disassociated things. But blunder in the relation between two cultures has immediate, practical, and terrible effect; blunder in the interaction of the New World with the Old may lead to catastrophes. These will be checked, modified, and even in part averted if the habit shall arise of appreciating, even in some measure, the real disassociation here of things apparently associated.

Hints of what we of Europe certainly need in this matter to-day, and of what America also needs (though less: for in America the Contrast is better recognised) are beginning to creep in. Public men are beginning to say—quite lately—that the use of one European language in America, the English, out of so many European languages, is a source of error, because it masks the essential division between America and *all* Europe. That is true; and the more that is said the better. Phrases expressing the truth are already appearing, though as yet they are very rarely put into print for certain reasons which I will deal with later. These phrases show an appreciation through the senses, a direct, personal appreciation of the gulf. Such phrases are not complimentary upon either side, and I therefore hesitate to quote them; yet will I quote four within my own recent experience. With ample apology, wringing my hands, and assuring every reader upon either side—supposing, that is, I find any readers at all—that they are not the phrases I would myself have used: carefully emphasizing my own judgment of their falsity, I will quote those four phrases for the sake of their strong testimony.

An American said to me, and I remember his words: "The trouble with you English is that you're dumb." Now, the word dumb, so used by an American, connotes a number of qualities of which difficulty in expression is the least. It connotes a blurred and inhibited mind. It would be true of the English were they American. It is not true of the English being English. It is a forcible little monosyllable, and it undoubtedly expresses the exact impression this American had received.

Very many Americans have said to me quite lately, with regard to Europe as a whole, "You don't seem *able* to clear up the mess you've made over there." That phrase is characteristic and the operative word in it is "able." It expresses the concrete lack of contact between the two sides of that very wide sea. If you were to say of two men playing chess, "They don't seem able to get the board into a regular pattern," that would be an exact parallel.

The two European phrases which I will quote are just about as flattering. The one is a printed phrase which you will find in the accurate and scholarly works of Mr. Max Beerbohm, who more than any man writing in the English tongue picks his expressions to correspond exactly with his thought, and succeeds. He wrote and published, speaking of the Americans, this: "They (the Americans) are as different from us as Hottentots." It is an extreme form of an idea which, less violently put, I have heard hundreds of times in the lips of Englishmen and others in Europe. And the other equally unflattering phrase was used to me by an European soldier of the continent, and this also everyone in Europe has heard a thousand times: "They (the Americans) are like children."

Now take those four operative words, "dumb," "able," "Hottentot," "children." They are all four wildly wrong.

No one with a knowledge of the two sides

could hear them without a laugh at a speaker or writer so wildly wrong. To say that the English are "dumb" is like saying that steel is "fragile." To say that Europe in the present great struggle is not "able" to clear up the mess "it" has made is (what I said in my parallel), like saying that two chess players do not seem "able" (collectively able by a common effort) to arrange their pieces in a regular and pretty pattern upon the board. To say "The Americans are as different from the English as Hottentots" is like saying that water is as different from wine as is vinegar, or that gold is as different from marble as is sewage. To say that the American intelligence and powers of appreciation are like those of "children" is like saying what Voltaire said when he called the genius of Shakespeare a monster. If I put it like that I shall perhaps help to apologise for the horrid rudeness of all four typical judgments. But all four are strongly illuminative of the separation between us.

Here are four typical sayings to which not only can I myself bear witness, but which, in their general character, are familiar to millions in speech, though very rarely printed. They *do* express what two opposed worlds are thinking: and they are each hopelessly off the mark. Why? What does their absurd irrelevance

prove? *That the sayers (American and Europ-
pean) were each dealing with wholly alien material.* That each sayer had suffered an earthquake
of experience and had reacted to it with what the
French called "a cry from the heart." Each had
thought to meet one thing and had met something else, startlingly, abominably, unlike his
expectation. Each had violently expressed his
alarmed indignation of surprise.

There is not in the modern world a body of
men with a greater command of expression, with
more knowledge and instinct when to plant each
expression, than the English. It is their genius.
It is their mark. It is their strong suit. The
English beyond all other men in Europe have
their imagination constantly at work, and they
are constantly clothing it with action. They are
the least "dumb" (in the American sense of
that word) of all Europeans.

Again; as to the "mess" and "cleaning it up."
Europe to-day is an exceedingly complex inter-
locking conflict, wherein one of two cultures,
Protestant and Catholic (but each main side
subject to innumerable variations and internal
divisions) is slowly grappling with the other.
From the smallest sub-unit to the largest group,
intelligence in Europe to-day is consciously
pitted against intelligence, tenacity against tenacity, will against will. It is, if one can use so

simple a metaphor for so multiple a thing, a
wrestling match, where both antagonists are on
the ground, innumerable muscles in each are at
play, and neither has yet touched with both
shoulders.

Again, the special difference between the
Englishman and the American has no relation
to the differences between the Englishman and
any other group of men, let alone the absurd
and remote Hottentot. There is nothing in common here except the mere factor of difference,
and the true phrase should be: "They are wholly
different from us, *but in a fashion not comparable to other differences.*"

Or again, the word "child."

The American way of appreciating, approaching, judging the alien European thing, or, indeed, anything novel with which he is brought
in contact, has nothing in common with imperfec-
tion, such as is connoted by the word "child."
It has three qualities which struck the speaker
of that very common, and most erroneous European judgment, but they struck him quite
wrongly. It has the qualities of simplicity, directness and elimination: the combined result of
these qualities grossly misleads the foreign observer. The American meeting with a problem
will (as anyone who knows the Americans, however slightly, can testify) reduce that problem

at once to its simplest terms, try to get to the
core of it. He will then concentrate upon it,
and for the purpose of concentration he will
eliminate all its variables, although he knows very
well that the variables are there. His process is
that of the mathematician or of the student of
physical science, and he pursues his own method
more thoroughly than any other kind of man I
know. That is why, I suppose, he solves his
own problems, the only problems he is called
upon to solve, with such astonishing rapidity and
success. A child does none of these things.
The difference between the American method
and ours is not the difference between immatur-
ity and maturity: it is the difference between one
highly mature method and another: the difference
between a mechanical and an organic method.

All these errors have been made, and a thousand others; all point to the Contrast.

Now to illustrate that Contrast further and
to examine its character in these pages I must
take a relative order in observing its manifestations. It is difficult to choose this order, because
it is quite impossible to say where the main
causes lie, and almost impossible to say which
cause comes first in magnitude or intensity.

I propose to take this order, in default of a
better.

First, very briefly, the Physical Contrast

which underlies the whole; next, at far greater
length, the Social Contrast—the contrast in
those daily human relations which are the small
external symbols of deep-seated spiritual motives producing them; as I speak of these I shall
try to discover that very essential thing, the
rhythm of action, the difference between one
body of men and another in their use of time and
space. I shall deal also with a sharp particular
point on which Europe makes one of its worst
errors, the American measurement by standards
of money.

Next I shall take the Political Contrast: the
contrast in the conception of government. After
this I shall attempt (with difficulty) to examine
certain special influences on the American soul
which have both emphasised and coloured The
Contrast: the Religious, the Military, the Literary experience of the New World. I then
regard what must be to most men the chief problem: the foreign relations of the United States
and especially the relation with England. Would
that I could have seized, recorded, and made real
that first, that mysterious earthly influence for
which we moderns have no name, but which the
wise ancients called Genius Loci: the Creative
Spirit of the Place: that which really, though
hiddenly, moulds men and things and makes us
all the children of our own land. But this is a

thing which escapes definition, and cannot be expressed save in rare flashes of verse or music, and then is rather glimpsed than expressed.

When I have ended the thesis, I shall have presented what will seem to most of those who had the patience to read me fantastic, to many absurd, to a few incomprehensible, but I shall have said a thing which I know to be true, and, being unusual, worth saying.

For truths are divided into two kinds; those with which all are familiar and which are therefore not worth saying, and which men repeat in the most horrible abundance from a sort of fatigue: and those other truths which men have not yet accepted, and the saying of which is, therefore, at once irritant and all-important.

To occupy (or waste) one's energies in the telling of this second kind of truth, the unfamiliar and vital truth, may be compared to scattering but a handful of seed by night upon untilled land. The chances are that none of it will grow.

II

THE PHYSICAL CONTRAST

O F all elements to be presented in mere words
the physical element is the most difficult
to convey. In a sense it is impossible. For
physical effects upon the soul, and therefore
the body of man, such as those of soil and air
and other innumerable, as yet undefined, as yet
not measurable physical influences are of their
nature *present* things. They are primal. If
you have not felt them, you do not know them.
Presentment or attempted presentment will
fail. Moreover, the presentment of a foreign
country is a task of one sort; the converse, the
presentation of one's own country to a foreign
people, is a task of another. Now there is a
third task, much more difficult task, which is the
one I am now engaged upon without pretending
to success, which is the presentation of a violent
opposition between the two. I have to present
to A (who thinks of dogs as a sort of cat, because
he has never known dogs but only cats) and to
B (who thinks of cats as a sort of dog, because

he has only known dogs) the contrast of the dog and the cat: not easy!

For that external world, that nature of soil and tree and landscape, in which the American soul has been formed, is as removed from the Old World as is one living species from another. This side of the Deserts at least, all the vast Central Valley (or plain), all the Eastern Atlantic Coast, is so alien to us in its form and inward character of land and water, and all that land and water bear, as to make an inexplicable thing. No one of European blood could here, in America, repose.

When a European first lands upon the eastern shores of the North American Continent, what strikes him?

If he is a man bemused by print, the grand transformer of our days, he will be struck, of course, most consciously by things of which he has read in print at home. If he is more happily fated, and feels direct impressions (young men have a better chance in this than their elders and the unlettered than the literary), the intense, the appalling novelty will produce an impression never to be removed from his mind: and if he travel over wide spaces of the New World in his first few days he is lucky, for it is the first hours of a foreign impression that leave the deepest mark.

The first thing that he will *then* notice is a nature violently different from his own habitat. He will not notice the particular points by which the shocks acts: he will receive as a whole a picture enormously foreign. The air he breathes is of a different quality. The horizons are of a different quality. He will not, as he does at home in Europe, passing, say, from the Mediterranean to the north, compare clear vision with blurred, or a sharp sky-line with distant haze. He discovers something much more startling: That the sharpness of the horizon is of a different kind, the mist other; the aspect of distant things has a new effect upon him, not what they gave in Europe.

If he is careful to note particulars, he will, as he comes first through country regions (for he will land in a city), observe that the trees are on another plan; their lines lead upwards, they are less of a foison, they are more repetitive. He will observe (though that is in part an effect of culture not of nature), a much larger proportion of dead or dying trees among them. He will observe that they are much more sparse, that they stand at more regular intervals; that they have, as a rule, much less undergrowth. He will observe, in a word, that the phrase "a wood," which he had thought, in the literature he has left behind, to refer to the whole world, referred

as a fact to Europe; the picture called up by the
same word to men of this New World is a picture of another kind. He will further observe
the perpetual similarity in that growth, which
sweep of common type he may call monotonous
or majestic according to his mood, but which, at
any rate, he will not match in his experience of
home. The only things that will a little remind
him (but in an odd way) of his past will be the
pines—and of these he will not see many if he
comes in by the usual entries.

Next he will note a difference in the waters.
They seem less contained, less sharply separated
from the dry land. Most of the rivers he first
crosses are either arms of the sea or tumbles of
stream, very shallow for their width, and of uncertain margin. I heard a European say: "An
American river is only a lot of water that happens to be there." I heard an American say:
"Your European rivers look as though they
had been laid out." And indeed the waters,
which are the life of landscapes, do thus belong
to two separated worlds. The Ohio at Cincinnati
runs in its gorge of promontory wooded hills.
But it is no more the Meuse than a steel engrav-
ing is a mezzotint.

What will most impress him will be the difference of outline in landscape: the folds of land,
like the woods, are more similar, more repeated,

and of a simpler sweep. The first mountains
which he crosses as he goes westward (unless he
touches certain exceptions, near the Hudson and
in New England) are slow lifts of land like succeeding waves: but not bold waves. These parallels are in no way the parallels of the Jura,
with their precipices and their endless diversity
of detail. They are rather a simple series of
folds, like what he has hitherto seen in water
but never yet in earth: a series of folds as like
one to another as the succeeding swells of a calm
sea. And their strange similarity is heightened
by the clothing common to all. The same sparse
and regular and short uplifted trees everywhere;
the branches rejected from the soil.

When he has crossed the mountains, he finds
for day after day of travel a country of the same
odd genus as that upon the eastern side of the
watershed. It is an illimitable succession of
flattish lands on which, again, the "Y"-branched
trees stand at random, more clear here than
there, but everywhere—to his European eye—
haphazard. These endless flattish lands are
carved very regularly into more or less deep
(never very deep) water courses of the same
sort as those he has passed, shallow for their
breadth, of uncertain margin, the level rising and
falling perpetually; a wide belt of uncertain
land, flooded or dry after flooding, their normal

accompaniment. He reaches the main such channel upon which all converge; he crosses it at any one of the crossings on the Mississippi or the Missouri, and save for some not striking difference in the scale, the impression made on him is that of crossing any other of these central depressions with their streams. There is the same adjunct of marsh, of occasional low, crumbling cliff, and, beyond, the same shallow valleys and the same arrangement of the trees.

He has, by this time, passed through as much space as separates Slavonic Europe from the Atlantic, or the Baltic from the Mediterranean, Warsaw from Paris, Naples from Hamburg: yet all the while his impression has been *one*. Of our European diversity not a trace: all one mood in nature and the world. Gradually as he goes yet further westward the landscape changes, but not with a physical frontier such as those which in Europe mark out with a sharp edge the many provinces of our mosaic. It is simply the dying out of the trees. At last, after a very wide belt of empty plains continually rising, he sees, not very conspicuous, through the thin air the first bare central mountains.

Here there is indeed a transition. But it is not the transition from plain to mountain which he has known in the Old World. It does not give him the air, the impression of what he has called mountain land. There is something deserted about it and also confused. The plain-platform of these gaunt and to him often shapeless hills is already half their height above the sea, so that their full stature is wholly dwarfed. The Rockies from the plains look small. For days (if he is proceeding in a travel of normal leisure and not in haste) the maze of bare lift and fall continues. The vast plateaux of this mountain belt, immensely wide, are most arid, brackish water and alkaline or sour dust: a man might walk a lifetime here in a lunar landscape bereft of men. So he goes on. It would be more than a month for a man on foot, it is days for a man on rails—this sterility of desert hills and cliffs and muddy melting snows. Then, in one miraculous moment, he and his world are changed. He reaches, unexpecting it, the sharpest border-line, the sharpest physical frontier that is, perhaps, in this world. For he comes to the high edge of the deserts, looks down as from a table, and passes at once into what stabs him with a sudden vision of Europe glorified.

It is the cascade of dense forests downwards and still downwards and, below, into the paradise of California. It is the Pacific.

*   *   *   *   *

If his journey takes our European to the

north after his landing on the eastern seaboard, the same endless repetition meets him of river, trees and plain; the same (to him appalling) *alien* monotony: at last it grows into spaces of naked rock: day adds to day without change. He comes upon those vast emptinesses of water, which are not at all like the sea although there is no land to be perceived beyond. And if he crosses these he comes to things more and more arctic, and at last to the abandoned waste of the hellish cold—in its brief summer a steam of mosquitoes and tepid waters.

If he goes southward he comes to luxuriance, but luxuriance not his own; the hills at first higher with some hint of abruptness, the grasses more rank. Till at last, under the influence of a sea almost tropical, he is in a region of the densest undergrowth: of creepers and mosses, vapours and great swamps; westward of this again are deserts more torrid, where the cactus throws its rare stunted shadow under a sun high, small and intense. These burning, naked sands and soft rocks stretch as widely as a great realm; they seem, to him of Europe, un-inhabitable. A scattered few attempt to use them in a fashion to him unaccountable. They are not a countryside.

Everything that he has seen to the north or to the south or in that more common western trajectory is utterly alien, until, after the last desert, he enters the true Californian land.

*   *   *   *   *

I know very well that these few lines give but a ghost of the reality: a very faint echo of that crash which the change of hemisphere thunders upon the sense. No written page thus trying to convey an alien landscape to the eye which has not seen it can give that vision, still less the alien air. I am sure that no page of mine will so convey them. But it is better to present so slight a hint of reality than to follow the appalling conventions of literature in these affairs, and the nothingness of routine falsehoods, of routine negligibles.

When first I came over the Alps into Italy I marvelled why, in all I had read of Italy, no one had told me that the houses were coloured, that a vast number of them were splendid palaces of towering sculptured stone, that the people walked with a free carriage and a nobility of demeanour superior to any others in Europe; and had a look confident and direct, which expressed the nobility of their blood. I marvelled that no one had told me in books of Italy save as a show place, in some way degraded. I marvelled that no one had hinted at what I now, arriving in Italy as a young man, *saw* to be the

certain promise of a coming Italian power. I
marvelled also, that I should have read in no
book of the turbidness of every Italian river
(save in its highest springs) of the dusty, uncertain earth which clothes the Apennines, of the
omnipresence of marble in the great buildings.
No book had given me this. The more pleasure
had I in the novelty of all I saw. But still I
wondered that no book should have given it to
me. The books had told me plenty of things
about Italy which purported to be revelations,
but were indeed only repetitions. Thus they
had talked of Italian skies: but those skies are
the same as ours in the north; our brilliant summer days in England, save that their intense
light is more permanent, are the same as the
much more numerous brilliant Italian days. The
books had talked of a general popular singing
in Italy: but singing thus is common everywhere
in Europe, save where the industrial blight has
atrophied mankind. They had talked of a multiplicity of beggars, whom I did not see; and of
brigands, who were not.

Not one of them, however recent, had repre-
sented Italy to me as it was.

It was the same with Spain when first I
crossed a pass in the Pyrenees and stood upon
an outlying rock and saw before me the burnt
waste of old Aragon. Why had no one told me

of landscape which would thus seize me as a new thing? It was a landscape with hardly a tree, a landscape of brown immensities, flat, or rolling, or leading up into distant high ridges which were as sharp as the nearest things, although a man could not reach them in three days.

It was the same in Africa when first I set foot upon the shores of Barbary. Why had no one told me that the sun was there something inimical, quite different, not the too strong friend he was in the islands or further European shores of that inland sea? For the sun is a too strong friend in Italy, in Spain; but in Africa an enemy.

It was the same in Russia, when, during a few days of research, following the campaign of Napoleon, I asked myself why no one had told me in some book of this spread land?

It was the same when I first came to my first modern German town. I asked myself how was it that, while books told me of their cleanliness, of their exact ordering, and the rest—matters of degree in all towns—no one had told me of the appalling, the insane, the nauseating new German architecture, which was different in *quality* from all else in Europe, and the decisive mark.

Much more did I as a boy, long before I had seen Spain or Italy or Africa or the appalling German towns, in the shock of the Narrows on

entering New York Harbour and the greater
shock of landing, ask myself, "Why did no book
tell me this, nor even any traveller?"

Well, I have attempted it in words, but, as
I said, only journeys a-foot and in early manhood flood the mind with reality.

Such journeys, I think (and I made them as
a boy), teach men The Contrast better than any
other experience. If they are made at once on
first landing and allowed their full immediate
effect they convince of The Contrast for
ever. Europe and America are two systems,
universes, creations, standing apart.

*   *   *   *   *

The works of man are mysteriously consonant
with the soil from which they spring. The
large similarity of the American soil has bred a
similarity in man's act upon it. The American
notes I know not how many differences of origin
and type in his own land; to the European foreigner the mark is, even in man's work, only one
of repetition. And this I take to be a proof of
the abyss between the New World and the Old.
We look all alike to Chinamen: Chinamen to us.
So this new society is in its own eyes multitudinous, in ours simple and undifferentiated.

The same towns, large or small, repeat (in
our judgment) the same rectangular pattern,

the same furniture seems to us to stand under
the same walls, the same transport clangs in
the streets; the same food, the same hours, the
same greetings, the same sounds, are (to the
foreigner) all he can discover. That similarity
(as we think it) has, I am told, even invaded the
garden of the Pacific. It was not so half a life-
time ago, in the days I knew as a boy.

Over all this reigns a climatic air, which no
less assures the European that he has come to
another world. Abrupt passages from mildness
to a sudden violent, burning cold, follow, not
with change of latitude nor with the rise and
fall of the sun, but with great sweeps of wind.
Through the mechanism of modern knowledge
the advent of each abrupt revolution is an-
nounced. The visitor reads under a warm sky
that to-morrow will be bitter with twenty degrees
of frost. He is startled to find that high noon
comes severe and wintry after a dawn of warm
weather. The curve of season has nothing in
it regular, swelling and unbroken. It is a pattern of zigzags shooting in vivid angles.

Now, all the life of the millions who live under
this vast caprice of extremes is moulded by it:
all their character and inmost part is affected.
Nor is this *régime* of abrupt strokes from ease
to violence the only, nor even perhaps the main,
external pressure making Americans what they

have become. Underneath it all there is a quality
not to be defined save, perhaps, very imperfectly
by metaphor; it is the quality which I will call
metallic: that is the adjective rising in the mind
of the European traveller wherever he goes between the Sierras and the Atlantic, the Arctic
and the Gulf.

A travelled European, knowing his own
world, is familiar with the discovery of unexpected things; with the advent of the heavenly
Italian air when he has passed the Alps; with
the new hard "feel" of the Baltic plain after the
German mountains, with the call of huge, rolling
flats in the Slavonic lands beyond, of the wooded
and sublime Scandinavian solitudes, of the
amazing aridities of Spain at its centre and of
the green "Huerta" all around the borders of
the Spanish Sea. But such novelties of experience within his own European air are nothing
to the novelty of America. There was in his
own air something common which he thought to
be of the whole world. He finds that it is not
of the whole world at all, but of Europe; and
that this other immensity to which he has come
needs, to express it, words which the European
tongues do not possess.

The Physical Contrast may or may not be
the most important factor in that general contrast which it is my business to express, and to

make certain, for those who read me. Physical conditions have something to do in the moulding of men, but only something. That the New World might have made other men with other material of tradition we discover by observing the French Canadian culture, for instance; a thing apart; and there are within the United States sharp differences which have arisen from causes independent of material environment. But the Physical Contrast is that urgently to be proposed, because it is that which the literary convention of our time has for some reason refused to acknowledge.

The humble, the illiterate, whose impressions are sound and undisturbed by the fictions of print, bear witness to that physical contrast perpetually. I know not how often I have heard from such exiles in their various tongues the phrase, "This is not like our own air," "This is not inborn." In old age they become like ghosts eager for living again. They have found America to be a world so removed from that of their origins, they have fallen under the possession of powers so diverse from, so unconnected with, the innumerable external things subtle or obvious, which created the European, that the European attempting to live in the New World has been appalled. There has resulted from the clash of those two factors—a race slowly made,

through millenniums under one air and coming
to be constrained, or rapidly remade under another—the quite new race of the New World:
a new race the fate of which, to survive or to die,
we know not: but a new race.

The human element, the physical type, the
American-bred man and woman are *a new thing*.

Here The Contrast is so violent that all perceive it: no hypocrisy, no snobbish pretence, no
political pretence or much commoner mere
acceptation of repeated nonsense is here of avail.
The Anglo-maniac of New York, the patient
civil servant of London toiling for an alliance
with America, the continental journalist writing
rubbish about "Anglo-Saxons," has here a
rock of glaring physical fact compared with the
solidity of which the smoke of all such fog is
insignificant. No one of them is in the least
doubt whether he is meeting an American or a
European. No servant in any hotel from Seville
to Warsaw is in any doubt whether the man
dining is American or European: no negro in
any Pullman car between Seattle and Palm
Beach has a moment's hesitation. The very
noodles who, born among the Eastern rich, and
living on Eastern rentals, desire to be taken for
Englishmen are still nervous after the longest
rehearsal of that wretched make-believe.

The American-bred type is wholly distinct. It is more distinct from anything in Europe than are the European types one from another. You cannot be certain, save in exceptional cases, before you hear him speak whether a man of breeding is Italian or English. You can not, perhaps, *always* be certain that one of the same class in the same company is American: for good breeding is a solvent; but you are certain in most cases. When it comes to portraiture the thing is beyond question. No one seeing in an English magazine the photograph of General Pershing, of the late Mr. Harding, or of Mr. Bryan could mistake any of those different faces for anything but an American face. An American face in the photograph of an English or French country-house party stands out at once. The portrait of the American celebrity of the moment, man or woman (particularly woman), appearing in our European Press is unmistakably national. The American face is as much a reality as the American weather, and, if there were no other, the physical contrast in features alone would be conclusive of my contention here.

But there is much more: there is gesture, voice, walk—all the externals of man; the change has come with a rapidity which makes it certain that the future differentiation will be far greater.

It will be, in some few generations, a continental difference openly marking two clearly distinct races. It seems also to prove that it is above all America, the American land, which has made the Americans: the soil and the spirit of that long-awaiting empty world have now stamped their own.

*   *   *   *   *

Such is The Contrast in its most intimate, its most real, its most undeniable form: the physical forms of land and men.

No wonder that it is a revelation to the traveller from the Old World! No wonder that he gropes for words in which to set down the transformation! The wonder rather is that every one has not appreciated, or rather taken for granted, the depth of the chasm that lies between this novel apparition and ourselves.

But though a vocabulary has not arisen to express the thing nor the habit of its expression yet grown, reality will be stronger than convention; and by the effects of The Contrast, that Contrast will imperatively convince mankind of its reality. We in England were more accustomed to the shock of the difference because a common language had long emphasized that difference. But all Europe is now beginning to know it (the war did that), and the sooner and

the better it is known the easier the relations
between these two quite separated worlds will be.

All the troubles we have had between us and
the worse ones we may yet have spring from an
attempt to mask that truth.

III

THE SOCIAL CONTRAST

THE adjective "social" is used at large, has grown diffuse, and has branched out with many meanings. My brethren of the Press use it as meaning "of wealthy women." I use it here in the strict and original sense to mean the relations between the citizens of one community, their general relations: that way of men with men which marks a national spirit. The contrast in this spirit between the American civilisation and our own is the first, the most universal, the most characteristic form of contrast to be grasped.

What is the essential mark of the American social spirit?

Its essential is publicity: the spirit of the market-place. The contact of individual with individual is indefinitely more continuous and more frequent in America than east of the great water, on the further shore. This all-pervading publicity comes from a different, an American, spring of the mind: a new, an American cause:

with a thousand effects. To that cause I will come later; but at first I note its most obvious effect: the mark of publicity.

To us Europeans rudely surprising, it is the note of all American things. It runs through every manifestation of American life and colours the whole. With us the market-place, the Forum, is a special meeting-place, privacy the rule. With the Americans the Forum is the habit of all life. In the Old World corporation stands separate from corporation, community from community, family from family, and the rest; among the Americans the sub-units, individuals, families, corporations, are possessed of a ceaseless molecular activity, as it were, and that especially of the individual; each affecting each directly and constantly. The interaction is perpetual between each man and his neighbours of whatever category of neighbourhood. It is a quality like that which our physical scientists put forward as their guess at the constitution of a gas, distinguishing it from that of a fluid, a violent rapidity of motion in the particles. It is the extension to the highest degree of what the great Greeks of antiquity called the *political* nature of man: his civic character. It is the extreme of what is much more falsely called, in a characteristically modern metaphor, the *gregarious* quality of man; not in the sense of men's tendency to act together in a great mass like a herd (though that is one secondary consequence of the thing), but rather in its tendency to make each man affirm his fellowship with his fellows.

For *intense individual contact and energy make for uniformity.* Let me emphasise that very important little paradox. There is no contradiction between the intensity of individual action and an almost mechanical similarity in general action. On the contrary, the two go together; and where the activity of the individual, his desire to depend upon himself and his consequent energy in action, are pushed to their furthest limit, there you will have also the most repeated contact between individuals, and, *as a consequence,* the most uniform result. That is why the uniformity of American life is so striking for the European observer.

Put a number of round smooth balls upon a billiard table. Give them each a slow and slight movement, and you will see no general movement appearing. There will be little clatter, few and rare collisions. Impart to them each a very rapid motion, that is, an individual intensity, and while you raise very greatly the noise of the shocks (which is a superficial phenomenon), and while you increase even more the number and frequency of collisions (which is the cause of the noise), you also soon develop a *resultant* of all

the random directions. If the sharp speed of
each be maintained you will soon perceive in the
movement of the whole a general swing, and all
that great mass of balls will be moving in a
crowd. So it is with a human society.

I am not here concerned with whether this
extreme of individual action and individual
activity, the consequent extreme of individual
contact (that is, of publicity), the further result
of large streams of common action and of a vast
uniformity also pushed to an extreme, are good
or evil; for it is not a judgment of good and
evil which I am attempting to describe, but a
particular social phenomenon; I do not judge
here, I only observe; and I say that the immediate mark, the obvious external mark, of America
as compared with our European selves is this
generalisation of the individual in action: his
presence everywhere in perpetual touch with his
fellows.

To us Europeans coming as travellers to
America the degree of the thing is so unusual
and, till it is experienced, so inconceivable that
it is the first shock of difference we feel between
ourselves and our hosts.

The American approaches and speaks to any
man anywhere without previous knowledge of
him, and is received as an Englishman, German
or Italian would receive a person he had known

all his life. In Europe even a man urgently
pressed to such action (for instance, a man
catching a train and not knowing his way to the
station) must always go through some form
before he addresses another man; and if there is
no urgency, the form must be prolonged and
careful. In America this form is unknown.
Contact is established at once and as a matter
of course; and we of Europe feel this strange
American thing subtly, and continually in the
ordinary approaches of men. One to whom you
speak in a shop when you ask him for goods, and
that one replying to you; one in a public office,
a post office, of whom you ask information and
who replies to you; one in any of a thousand
relations, which recur daily, treats you in
America after a fashion unknown in Europe;
and when people are honest with themselves,
their sharpest memory of the United States,
especially if they remain there (as do most
travelling Europeans) for but a moment of
their lives, is that brusque relation, vivid, not to
be mistaken; different from any experience in
their own world.

On most Europeans this novel relation acts
as an acute irritant. A smaller number it amuses.
To all it is enormously strange: to me attractive.
But to the American it is inconceivable that it
should be strange. It is to him as normal as

breathing. We call their mood a lack of privacy: they call our mood by equally uncomplimentary names. I have heard the thing deplored by some few Americans, but only by Americans of a leisured sort, and more often by men already acquainted with Europe. The mass of Americans have it of nature and take it for granted.

For instance, if a matter purely domestic becomes of sudden interest to the public at large, there is no indecency in printing it at large and commenting upon it as freely as the weather.

You find the same spirit (to quote an illuminating detail) in what is, to us, a pleasanter form, and yet what is at the same time the most vital superficial effect: the well-to-do man's idea of a home.

As the European visitor goes out of one of the great American cities and enters their miles of suburbs, where the wealthier men have built their houses, the startling thing to his eyes is to note that *there is no division between one man's ground and another's*—they all stand on one lawn! The startling thing that strikes his ears is the thunder of electric cars clanging past these houses on their steel rails all day—and all night. Wealth and opportunity in America connote the very opposites of what they do in Europe: extreme neatness, rarity of detail, an hospitable cleanliness of bath, drains, sinks;

facile communication, plenty of noise and metal
—and no seclusion. With us wealth, especially
wealth long possessed, is marked by an extreme
of seclusion; a horror of noise; a carefully acquired distance from communications; a good
deal of dust on old books and furniture; a mass
of detail in every kind of reading and picture
and chance-inherited or picked up what-nots by
the hundred; repose, and (especially with the
English gentry) what they call Froust—which
some of them also call Fug.

It is not newness which digs this chasm
between the two, for the American thing is
found in families and fields two hundred and
fifty years old; it is a fathomless spiritual gulf
separating two kinds of men and making it so
that in the world of the one the other could not
live.

Individuals support the change: but an English group, remaining English, *could not* (I say)
live in America: it would breathe an alien air
and die.

This element of publicity, then, is everywhere.
I could by way of paradox pick out a thousand
examples of the apparent contrary: things on
which American convention forbids discussion,
but European permits it, if not fully, more freely.
But these make no counter balance, for there are
an equal amount of conventions the other way

about: things not discussed in Europe freely but in America universally discussed: income, for instance, and digestion. But these examples of exception on the one hand, of exaggeration on the other, do not affect the main truths, that the note of American society is life under the eye and in the ear of all.

I have said that this root-character of vibrating individual activity leads not only to perpetual personal contact but also to *uniformity;* and I have said that there is here no contradiction, but that the one is an obvious consequence of the other.

This uniformity, this second effect of publicity, is as striking to the European as the first effect, that of perpetual contact. For the contrast here also in the matter of uniformity is bewilderingly intense.

Tocqueville, in his great book, now nearly a century old, remarked (but failed to explain) what were then the already apparent evidences of the thing. He said that, in some way which he found too difficult to analyse, the height of "freedom" in America (by which he meant the height of individual release from restraint), was accompanied by a strange universal sameness in action and doctrine. The whole crowd moved together: certain abstract doctrines were taken for granted as part of the nature of things, unquestioned and universal action of one strict pattern everywhere followed as a matter of course. To-day he might add that the spirit of uniformity had reached a mechanical level, and had on the foreign observer the effect of an engine perpetually repeating a limited and exact function. There is here, *perhaps,* another factor at work besides publicity, which factor is a combination between the directness of the American mind (a projection of its simplicity) and the nature of the opportunities it finds.

In Europe the epigram passes round, "Everything in America is upon a belt," by which I suppose the author of it meant that the European observes in America a lack of that high differentiation to which he is accustomed in his own world. Now the American, of course, is awake to a set of domestic differences which the foreign visitor does not feel. He marks the great difference in spirit between one of his cities and another, between one of his social classes and another. But if he will compare the social manner of his own country with that of Europe he will, I think, agree with me that there is in his society not only uniformity of ideas (compared with ours), but also a widespread uniformity of lesser daily action.

The rapid vibration of individual life has not led to a multiplicity of private habits as a slower

but progressive individual pace might have done.
It has led to the contrary. It has rendered the
individual typical: a common mould exists into
which men are run and their surroundings.
Thus the large hotel is of identically the same
structure, plan and end wherever you go in the
United States; and if it be objected that the
hotel is naturally so, being an institution made
to be in common and universal, one may reply
that nothing in Europe is more personal and
"each-of-its-kind" than our inns. One may add
that the human house in America is equally on
a pattern, its furniture, its reading, the very
details of warming and of cooking and the rest.
Every nation, and for that matter every civilisation, has some uniformity in such things. There
is a French house which is not Italian; an European house which is not Asiatic. But in America
uniformity is far more striking (for it is far
more exact) than it is with us. It has a far
sharper edge, it makes a far neater imprint, it
is far less varied within its own genus. And the
converse is true; the traveller is certain of find-
ing one limited set of things everywhere; he is
equally certain of lacking others. He will find
the same book, the same bath, the same radiator.
He will not find Chambertin or, say, *"Lepanto"*
—a poem, or changing soft songs. He feels
a regimental effect.

Upon this I know not how many other causes converge, besides those I have guessed at—the even topography; the rapid spread of population over a vast area, still continued in a flood and destined to continue; the delight in mechanical application.

Let me illustrate this last point. It is found that a particular activity, mental or physical, say the picking of books out of a library, or the moving of the human body from a lower to a higher place, is done at a certain expense of energy. A newly proposed system of indexing saves, in the first case, a proportion of that energy compared with an earlier system of indexing. A novel form of transport, the American elevator ("lift" in English), saves a proportion of energy compared with an earlier form, a staircase. In our European world the earlier form will nearly always survive—not precariously survive: not slowly die out, but *survive;* continue, outlast the innovation—and that stubbornly: so will also many other forms earlier still. This tenacity in the survival of old instruments goes with the spirit of privacy, with the individual private, domestic, turned inwards; with the unit of the corporation, of the college, of the family, also turned inwards.

And with us such differentiation is not due to dulness or routine, but just the opposite. It is

a mark or symbol *in our society,* of those who
hold a special and even a superior place therein.
Thus the high Western civilisation of France,
Spain, Britain, Italy is far more differentiated
than that of Prussia, Russia or the Balkans.
With the Americans it is the reverse. Old forms
surviving mean, there, something sluggish or
poor: an inhibition. To have things about one
less "efficient" than those of the past is, among
Americans, a sign of weakness. Many a European library is proud to be so individual as to be
arranged haphazard: to allow a man to browse
among its books at the expense of their continual misplacing. Its members choose by discovery, and find the pleasure of such a freedom
to exceed the pleasure of rapid delivery through
exact order. And in such old European libraries a change of system, the closing of the shelves
to such general inspection for the sake of exact
order, would be thought a loss, not a gain. But
in America the consequent disorder would be
found intolerable. Again: many a rich man,
most rich men, I think, in Europe, will choose
to have staircases in their houses, and will not
have a lift (or elevator): if they do admit the
new thing they only do so in a sort of servile
way to spare labour for menials, but not as a
luxury for themselves. That is an attitude with
which, no doubt, a number of men in America

may sympathise, but which America as a civilisation rejects. The saving of energy in any department is (in America) a progress. To waste energy for the sake of individuality, caprice, elbow-room, tradition, is, with Americans, to be eccentric and *less* than their standard.

This spirit of common action takes the form also of creating enormous markets even for the things of the soul. It creates on a huge scale and as a *benefit* what our urban centres in Europe also suffer from not a little, as a curse: the "Best Seller": the book which spreads like fire through dry grass, not because it makes any special appeal to individual minds but because a crowd takes it up. Only some one book can at the same one time thus capture the universal market, but almost any book may do so. One book among a myriad gets the lead (no one knows how) and, immediately, its competitors fall out, and that one book sells by the million for three months *and is forgotten in six*. That is the astounding part of the affair. The appetite admits itself worthless in judgment and abdicates immediately.

This spirit of common action shows itself much more importantly in the realm of ideas, from which all material manifestations spring. Social Doctrines are in America universal. Thus one social doctrine—the treatment of all religious

statement and practice *within a certain limit* as
private opinions, the persecution of all beyond
that limit as intolerable—is universal. It is unquestioned. It is taken for granted. No one
may be specifically burdened for rejecting (or
accepting) the Catholic doctrine of clerical celi-
bacy. But no one will be tolerated who denies
the Catholic doctrine of monogamy.

Again, the value, sacredness and efficacy of
the vote: here is an example of that which should,
perhaps, more properly belong to an examination of American political conditions, but which
may be brought in here. The conception that a
majority[1] has a divine right to decide in any
matter is universal in America, not as a conclusion of reason but as an accepted dogma. It
is not the doctrine that society as an organism
may impose its organic will—*that* all humanity
accepts: it is the doctrine that majority voting
expresses that will!

The principle is, as all will agree after a moment's thought, absurd. It only applies when
three rare conditions are all present together.
(1) Universal interest, (2) a common experience, (3) a perfect machinery. Shall two lads
of twenty-one and twenty-two outvote their

---

[1] The Constitution does, in effect, often give a minority
power, *e. g.,* through the Senate. But the majority doctrine is unquestioned.

father? Is a family less of a social unit than a
minx? Do one million care (or know) more
about bimetallism than 999,999? But the case
is even worse than such unanswerable questions
imply. It is clear to reason that such a conception, even if its principle be admitted, must have
physical, necessary, limits. Society could not be
conducted at all, and the State could no longer
exist, if fifty-one out of a hundred were in all
matters whatsoever free to dictate to forty-nine.
It would be impossible mechanically, because the
number of things to be decided is infinite. It
would be intolerable in morals, because it may
well be (and usually is the case) that the great
majority are slightly opposed to something to
which the minority is passionately attached: for
instance, the Mass.

In a word, it is self evident that majority rule,
even if you accept it as a divine doctrine, as
something in the very nature of morals, can only
work on a small field; right or wrong, it can
only act over very restricted areas. Yet the
limits, until very lately at least, have only been
accepted subconsciously in America; only recently has Europe noticed the beginnings of an
American discussion upon them, which discussion had hardly begun when I was a young man
in America thirty years ago.

It is perhaps the policy of Prohibition that has

raised the issue of majority rule. I do not know.
But, I repeat, the discussion has come. It will
lead far; but it will not shake that conception of
the divine right of a majority. That is a universal idea in America, rooted in the public mind and
as omnipresent as was in other times and places
the right of the Church to impose itself exclu-
sively in, say, the English world of the thirteenth
century.

Philosophers have, of course, debated the matter of majority rule both in America and in our
own civilisation, and that long before the modern
organisation of voting upon a very large scale
was known. They at once discovered that the
right of a majority thus to dictate can be based
upon nothing but the absurdity of its alternative.
If the majority has not the right to coerce the
whole, still less has a minority. Supposing a
complete identity of units and supposing an
equality of interest in all those units, majority
rule is merely the statement that its opposite is
more absurd than itself.

But that impassive way of treating the idea
of decisions by majorities is not at all the way
in which the American mind has received it. It
has been received as a self-evident truth in morals.

I know well enough that the wisdom of those
who founded the American Constitution checked
majority rule, limited it, and so saved the State.

But my point is that this dogma, so universal, so unquestioned, so foolish, is an example of *Uniformity*.

Another example of this uniformity of social action is found in the great waves of public feeling which sweep the New World. They change rapidly in direction and in object. That of to-day may be almost opposite in direction to that of to-morrow. The object exciting the wave of to-day may wholly differ in nature from the object exciting that of to-morrow: but the prime mark of *Uniformity* is never lacking. The vast mass of human beings moves as one body.

Such cohesive universal action is a most formidable instrument of power. Of all the characteristics of American life which Europe respects, calls upon as an ally or dreads as an opponent, this is the chief; and it is not unamusing to watch the clumsy efforts of European propagandists to produce these waves in the United States. Even as I write the opposing interests of the French and English are urging these peoples to attempt by print and missionary speakers the rise of such a wave; with France it takes the form of attempting to raise an enthusiasm for her sufferings, with England it takes the form of appealing for American entry into a "League of Nations," which it is hoped may be turned into an anti-French instrument. These attempts fail. For no force can raise these waves save one arising upon American soil. One European missioner will say, "Watch me! I am about to produce a universal enthusiasm over there for the League of Nations!" Another will say, "Watch me! I am going to stampede them into making the Germans pay." These efforts do not succeed, and their authors become ridiculous.

But when the source of an American enthusiasm is native it may have an astonishingly rapid rise and a still more astonishing vigour. I suppose no one will deny, least of all Americans conversant with their country as a whole, that the future has in store for us a succession of such enthusiasms. But it is characteristic of the situation that we in Europe never know what idea will arouse them nor whence it will spring. Such emotions come too suddenly for us Europeans even to note their origin. We do not understand their nature.

Among the universal ideas which in practice are thus everywhere accepted, and stamp the public mind of the United States, Europe has in particular noted one; and Europe (particularly England) has so misunderstood this one, that I hope to be excused if I attempt at some length to explain it. I mean the money standard: the close connection everywhere apparent in the

American mind between civic value and an individual accumulation of wealth: the use of *acquired* (not inherited) fortune as a test of worth.

There is no point on which more acrimonious folly has been talked by foreigners than this, and all that folly proceeds from a lazy, or ignorant or, at any rate, an imperfect analysis of the thing.

There is an attitude towards private fortune, the private possession of wealth, which is, exactly, *idolatrous,* that is, which (*a*) imputes to this dead thing living attributes, (*b*) worships that dead thing. For in these two errors combined does idolatry consist. Where that spirit of idolatry is present, where there is a worship of the wealthy man, where there is a confusion between the advantages of wealth and the objects proper for human admiration, there you have as base a corruption of the religious instinct as man can suffer. That is, *very* exactly, Mammon.

Now at the risk of appearing paradoxical and fantastic to nearly all European readers, and even to many American readers, I will boldly say that no modern society is so free from this detestable heresy as the American. To transfer admiration from the thing possessed to its possessor; to conceive that the mere possession of material wealth makes of its possessor a proper object for wor-

ship; to feel abject before another who is wealthier—such emotions do not so much as enter the
American mind. To say to himself, "That man
is an owner of great wealth: therefore I respect
him as I would respect a great poet or a great
soldier," is impossible to an American.

In Europe this mood of Mammon is never
absent. I am glad to say that even with us the
degrees vary in different places and different
times. It was very much worse before the war
in England than it is to-day. It was very much
worse just before the war than it was a generation earlier. It is worse in Paris than in any of
the French provinces, and worse in the French
provinces than in Italy. But throughout our long-
stratified European societies there is everywhere
a measure of this money-worship; and it is detestable. You may compare the beastly thing to
the smell of gas. A leak may be just strong
enough to be slightly unpleasant: or stronger
and very unpleasant; or appalling. In a few
places it will make a place uninhabitable and
cause death. Now to apply the parallel to Mammon, we in England live to-day complaining of
that smell of gas as pretty nearly intolerable.
Just before the war (which came in to correct
the thing) it really had become intolerable. We
were in a room where the leak was so bad that
it drove people out. All over Europe (even in

Castilian Spain, which is the freest of all our
societies from the horror) you can smell that
gas. In America you are wholly free from the
faintest odour of it.

Clear distinction is necessary in these things
as in all modern problems, for our modern words
have lost outline; yet according to whether you
use words accurately or not your moral conclu-
sions differ as black from white. Mammon is
not the passion for *getting* money, nor the desire
for what money *can buy;* still less is it the envy
of those who have more money than oneself. It
is the transference to the wealthy man of qualities not present in him and suggested only by
the fact that he is wealthy. It is expressed in
the feeling of genuine respect for a rich man and
genuine contempt for a poor one; in the attribu-
tion of virtue to the one and of vices to the other.
You will, I say, find that disease of the soul
less present in the United States than in any
other modern society. Mammon does not appear with the Americans in gesture, or tone of
speech or glance, nor in any of those things
which betray the deference of the soul. I, at
least, have never seen those glances, or gestures,
or heard those tones in America. With us they
are universal.

What, then, is it in the American attitude
which has been mistaken for Mammon?

It is something quite other. It is the three-fold conception (1) that success in accumulation connotes effort upon the part of any man; (2) that American opportunity should make this equally possible for any man; and (3) (negatively) that there is nothing else in the State either so easily measurable as the money-standard or so universally present.

The American sees civic life as a race, entry to which is open for all. Nature around him lies still largely unexploited; new ideas of its new use arise day after day. The race is, as a fact, entered by nearly all, and your place in it can be—very roughly—measured by your material achievement. It is natural that under such conditions such a test should be applied.

The simplicity of the standard has its evils, and they are gross. They lead to a difference between the idea of production and the idea of accumulation. They lead to an excess of cunning, though that, again, is cunning of a simple type. But these and many other defects attaching to the conception most emphatically do not include that disgusting, that degrading element of base personal worship: and the exclusion of this evil is well worth the admission of all the rest. As to the weak side of this "money-standard" habit, what else would you expect to find in a society which has had for its main temporal

task during three centuries the development of a
vast and still unexhausted continent? As to its
strong side, it is a credit to the civic sense of
Americans that they use it as they do without
admixture of false emotion.

There is proof that what I say is true. In a
society degraded by Mammon those qualities in
man which are inherent (from, say, Literary
Talent, which is among the lowest, to, say, Holi-
ness, which is the highest of all) are held to be
less significant than the mere possession of money.
They are more or less admired (and that in the
wrong order), but they are never worshipped.
Worship, to parody the theological definition,
"is reserved for Money alone." In societies comparatively free from the disease the inherent
qualities belonging to a man as man (talent,
courage, etc.) are, in their greater manifestations,
worshipped. Now among the Americans these
inherent qualities not only reach their right place,
but take, if anything, a place a little too high. A
great soldier having saved Europe on a salary of
five thousand dollars a year, the Americans are
moved to receive him as he should be received.
Did a poet appear now-a-days (the world is
waiting for him, but he has not come) the Americans would receive him as he should be received.
In London rich women would ask him to lunch;
but not the same rich woman twice. The poet

would, in London, be an exhibit and a trapping
at her table, like the ephemeral hero of the last
scandal. That is not true of America. Hostesses
scramble for lions there as here. But in America
the lion is more than the hostess. With us, unless the lion is the richer, the lion is the less.

Or again. Among people in one house-party
upon our side of the Atlantic degrees of deference are almost entirely determined by wealth.
A very rich man is, in such a party, a special
and sacred being, far more to his companions
than to the servants. A poor man is insignificant. Such is our chief vice. We see men
through an atmosphere or coloured screen of
possession. In America they enjoy the corresponding virtue of seeing men as they are. In
the midst of so much which spiritually weakens
the New World this virtue, which is part of its
candour, permanently strengthens it.

So much for the American money standard,
our European misconceptions on which have bred
so much false judgment as to merit this long
digression. That digression arose, it will be remembered, in connection with the effects of
American Uniformity.

Now in this matter of the moral effects of
American Uniformity two are worth noting before we leave it: an advantage, and a defect. The

advantage is a universal courtesy, the defect is assurance.

Courtesy in America never fails. It is found in all states of fortune and in all degrees of haste. That it has not our forms makes it, to those of us who care to observe, the more conspicuous. The great machine of American Uniformity needs such oil and gets it abundantly. In no community I know will you find a less number of proud, or surly, or neglectful men; for pride and surliness and neglect are the fruits of isolation. On the other hand, there is none in which assurance—that is, certitude based on insufficient evidence or on mere repetition—is more rooted: and it is a weakening thing to the individual man and to the State.

For example, each latest fad in the physical or historical jargon of guess work is accepted for gospel after a fashion far more universal than with us. With us it is a mark of intelligence and reading to ridicule the successive imaginaries which are presented to us for realities—The Cave Man, and The Nordic Race and all the rest of the ephemeral procession. To accept these things seriously and make them a basis for action or even thought is associated in the European mind with something imperfect in a man's training. I have even heard them called "Suburban" and "Middle-class" by middle-class people in the sub-

urbs; and when things get as far as that it is a
wonder and a sign. For instance, such ephemeral books as these, *Outlines of History* and
the rest, have about them, in the eyes of the cultured in Europe, something comic and absurd.
The musty, belated elementary "science" and
history of their authors, half of it already proved
wrong and the other half guess work, is a joke—
especially with the French, who are keenly alive
to the fun of such figures. But in America I
found that trumped-up stuff taken quite seriously.

With us in Europe the affirmations of pseudo
science in such books as these are a jest. But in
America the flood covers the highest mountains.
No man doubts. All accept as one, save isolated
groups who are *justly* ridiculed as *less* informed,
for *they* base their opposition not on better reading and clearer thought but on worse; *our* denial
of, say, the mass of German rubbish on the
Scriptures is based on a near familiarity with its
exposure, but *their* denial is based on Jonah and
the True Right Whale.

This assurance, doing harm within to the
American, is a domestic concern of his own;
doing harm in foreign relations it is the world's
concern, and in that field it might at any moment
do the greatest harm. To accept insufficient or
actually false stock phrases in Ethnology and

History is a bad thing for society, but to accept them in International Politics is ruinously dangerous, both to the accepter and the foreign object of his judgment. Words like "Caveman," "Natural selection," "Psychoanalysis," are one's own family affair, but "Anglo-Saxon," "Latin," "Nordic," "Self-determination," and "Militarism" may start a war.

Luckily, two powerful checks restrain the effects of these asphyxiating tenuosities: first, the Americans have a vivid and most healthy *instinct* against foreign entanglements; secondly, they possess a distinct, clearly-defined *tradition* against the same: a tradition derived from the great founders of the American Commonwealth and fixed in memorable phrases.

      *   *   *   *   *

I now come to a quality in the American social spirit which cannot be attached to any material cause, which is a product of I know not what virtue or happy accident in the origins of that society. To this quality one can only give the name of *Candour;* it is straightforwardness and unasking sincerity. It has a general effect (I know not for how long this effect may endure) of joy.

I have heard innumerable judgments passed upon the American people by Europeans. Most of these judgments, as is natural with aliens,

were unfavourable, and none were less favourable
than the judgment of the English gentry—
though the French and Italian gentry run their
English colleagues close in the attack on
America. But in all these judgments, favourable and unfavourable, unintelligent (as were
the great majority) or intelligent (as were a
rare few), there almost always appeared with a
note of envy, of surprise, of bitterness—or of
mere regret—the statement that the Americans
were happier than any people of the Old World.

They *are,* much happier. It is the astonishing
and outstanding thing upon the spiritual side
which no one seeing that people, and telling honestly what he has seen, can hide. They are the
happiest white people in the modern world.

Wherever you go in the whole of the vast territory of the States you discover that sort of
freedom in the soul which is the breeding soil of
happiness. I have said that I could discover no
cause—certainly no moral cause—for the Candour which is at the root of all this happiness;
but at any rate I am sure that the cause of the
happiness is Candour. The American people
live in truth.

By this I do not mean that they have not the
vices common to mankind, and the particular
vices common to our Western race, and the still
more particular vices which attach to their own

predominant doctrines. What I mean is that the perpetual habit of repression, accompanied by an indurated falsehood of expression, which runs through and through the governing classes of Europe, is absent; and I am fully confident that to the absence of such an evil we must ascribe that other good of a light heart.

I have spoken in another part of this essay upon the effect of candour in the matter of architecture, and in certain other social relations; but its chief effect is joy.

Now will this effect endure? I return to that question. About a year ago a German travelling in America for the first time, and saying what I say, that this note of joy had struck him most, added: "Nor is it marred by any foreknowledge of its own cessation. They do not know for how short a time this joy will last!"

I cannot pretend to this critic's prophecy. The joy may last or it may not; it cannot last for ever, it cannot last, indeed, for very many generations. Every civilisation that has developed upon this earth has passed rapidly enough from simplicity to doubt, and from doubt to despair, save indeed where it has been relieved, as was Rome in the fourth century, by that one sublime philosophy which can alone redeem us from despair, but cannot give us back our innocence. Every civilisation which has appeared upon this earth has either ended by accepting sorrow as a portion, or by rebelling against that human fate, and so destroying itself. But every civilisation has also passed through an early phase of full expression and satisfaction, and in that phase the American people are to-day.

So true is this, that with difficulty does any European man, acquainted as he is with the numerous and accumulated moral evil of the Old World, and haunted, as he must be (if he is of any sufficient culture) by the putrescent hypocrisies of those who are still, with us, in the tradition of government, convince Americans of how false our world is. With difficulty can he convince Americans with whom he holds conversation that Europe is what it is in the way of unhappiness and of deceit. How often has not an American friend of mine said to me, for instance in connection with the hopeless corruption of our public life, "Why don't they take it into the Courts?" fully believing as he said this that our judges were quite independent of the politicians! Fully believing that there was with us an active public opinion, as a natural and necessary part of any human society which would drive from office a minister caught taking a bribe! How often has not an American friend asked me which of two newspaper-boomed Parliamentarians of ours was the greater genius.

There is still in the atmosphere of the United States—and pray God it may long so remain!—a taking for granted of certain fundamental simplicities and sincerities in motive and action which we have overlaid with I know not how many traditional silences. Here in Europe, and particularly in England, a man who knows how government is now conducted since it ceased to be aristocratic feels himself in the presence of silent men furtively beckoning one to another. In America he knows himself to be in the presence of men speaking frankly and aloud. It is the difference between foul air and fresh.

It is later in this essay that I must touch upon the internal relations of the Americans with Europe, and upon their relations particularly with the old, hieratic society of Britain; but I will say here in passing, and before concluding this section, that in nothing do these relations work less easily than in the contrast between the American candour and its accompanying happiness, and our own secrecy with its accompanying despair.

I know very well there attaches to the latter a certain savour of antiquity and tradition, though I believe, for my part, that one can have that savour without the evil. I know that there is a curl of contempt against simplicity, but upon the balance, and having seen many men in many places, I for my part will give my vote for candour; for its fruit is happiness, and happiness is the end of man.

I will conclude this brief analysis of the Social Contrast with one other of those statements which I know will sound fantastic, or in the abused modern sense of the word, "mystical," and this also I am going to say because I believe it to be true. The American use of *time* and *space* is in high contrast with that of the Old World; by which I mean that the rhythm of life is other from our own in Europe; quite other.

Everything is in the mind. What men *think* of an hour or a hundred miles is the important thing in the making of their corporate lives. There are, indeed, modern fools who go on to tell you that what the mind holds of these things is all they are, and that they do not exist outside the mind. I will leave them at it. But without delay upon such follies it remains true that a society is wholly coloured by the effect of time and space upon itself: the way in which it uses, and is affected by, those dimensions.

Now, according as you use your time and space, and as they affect you, your *rhythm* is produced. A man who speaks at a certain rate, who in his work works half a day at a stretch, who in a short progress feels a great sense of distance, is under one rhythm. A man who speaks or thinks rapidly but otherwise has the same habits is under another rhythm. A man who speaks or thinks slowly but can work only at one thing in short bouts is under a third. The rhythm of a diverse action spread over many activities differs in quality from the rhythm of concentrated action upon one—and so forth. Well, in every character of social rhythm, in the wave-length and the elevation of the wave, and the oscillation-ellipse of the wave, and the cross-section of the wave, and the rate of the wave, and the matter of the wave, American life and thought contrast completely with those of Europe. Nothing in all the aspects of the general contrast is more conclusive to my thesis than this. Whether that contrast proceed mainly from material conditions (as many would say) or from deeper and unseen causes (as I believe), it is clearly present. Men upon both sides of the ocean express their sense of this continually, but do not, I think, as a rule express it accurately. The American is rather proud of asking the European whether he is not "rattled" and "hustled" by the speed of American life. The European complains, on that suggestion, of just the things suggested to him; and the American judging Europe will (of all adjectives!) use the adjective "slow."

Now, as I see the thing, these statements are not only simple but wrong. The great quality

of the American rhythm is shortness of scale as
applied to time and the opposite as applied to
space, compared with the European rhythm. The
American rhythm is more vibratory, the European more surging; there is in the one something
more metallic than in the other; there is in the
one something more mechanical and less organic.
I hear in one the sound of a hammer, in the other
wind through trees. Prolonged effort and effort
spread over many fields of life are less consonant
to the American air than to the European.

So much for time; but distance, space, has a
different effect upon the American mind, and an
opposite one. A man going from Paris to Rome,
a European, has a different spiritual experience
of space from that of a man going to New York
from Chicago. It is not a matter of frontiers.
A man going from London to Glasgow and back
subtly receives quite another effect of space from
one who takes the round-trip between New York
and Pittsburgh.

This other-use, other-relation of space comes
in by many unexpected ways. You are "in"
Chicago—a town of under three million—ten
miles from its centre either way—and more: I
do not mean only technically or legally within
nominal city boundaries, but under the same
conditions urban and of Chicago. Paris is much
the same. London is more than double. But

in twenty miles you traverse London from country-side to country-side, and Paris in far less.
You carry an American town out with you indefinitely into the country. *Space is less.*

And what is true of space spread out length-
ways is also true, somewhat, of space up and
down.   American height seems less high.
Height (on the east coast at least, and the middle
west) receives—in my eyes the same impress of
reduction: why, I cannot tell.

Testimony to such influences is difficult to
give: the modern world is warped by the idea
that exact measurement is the only source of
knowledge.   But the testimony is true.   Space
is not to the American what it is to us.   Beauvais
soars higher than the Woolworth Building, and
the Palace of Avignon is bigger than the Brook-
lyn Bridge.

This contrast in rhythm is a fundamental contrast and a permanent one.   If it changes it will
change only to increase.   It affects the whole of
life.   It has all sorts of odd side effects which I
perhaps exaggerate from the very fact of their
strangeness, but which are certainly there.

For instance, it affects the quality of repose.
The European rhythm demands longer and more
absolute repose: perhaps I should say repose of
a different kind.   The European will say that
the American city appalls him with its noise.   It

would be more subtle and nearer the truth to say
with the *quality* of its noise. I have used the
metaphorical word "metallic" of the New World;
it applies here. There is a difference between
noise metallic and non-metallic, and there is no
doubt whatever that the former is distressing to
one sort of mind and negligible to another, just
as there is a difference between dyes which may
be called mechanical and colours which may be
called vegetable, and the former are acutely irritant to one kind of man and negligible to another. Now the first kind of man is typical of
our side of the sea and the second of the other.
But this does not mean that mere repose is more
necessary to the European than to the American.
It is a matter of quality, not of degree. There
are forms of repose less necessary to us, more
necessary to them.

Here I am in deeper water, for one can talk
of oneself with security, of a foreigner one must
talk with hesitation; but it seems to me that the
"short" rhythm connotes repeated repose. If a
man is disturbed by a long and complicated process of thought, and craves rather for lucidity and
brevity, this, indeed, connotes a form of high
activity, but it also connotes a special form of
fatigue at the end of it.

Of this difference in rhythm I will give an
instance that comes home to all travellers across

the Atlantic. In common with most other recent
visitors I have noticed the effect of it in the con-
trasting forms of conversation between what we
have in Europe and what they have in America.
Five men illustrating in conversation some point
between them will in America develop five full
accounts and are listened to separately and in
turn. The pattern is one of five units spread
over a certain short space of time, with silence
for the listeners, no interruption, and an end of
the affair after a few such interchanges of fixed
and exactly limited expressions of thought. The
same point debated with us over a much longer
space of time uses a much larger number of units,
exceeds such limits, is filled with adventitious
allusion; and this contrast I take to be a function of the contrast in rhythms of which I have
spoken. For in the case of the European man,
whose habit is one of lengthy concentration and
correspondingly lengthy repose, the many aspects of a thing can be presented in many short
statements, subject to interruption which does
not mar the whole. Whereas the American man,
whose concentration is intense but brief, will
give all that he has to say, give it in a very limited
field, but that field fully covered. And I feel
no oddity in the apparent paradox that the
shorter American rhythm uses a more even intonation, a lesser vocabulary, a longer unit of

expression; the longer European rhythm more inflection, shorter individual speeches and the irruption of side aspects. The one seems to be a consequence of the other, for the European manner defers repose, the American secures it at more frequent intervals and ends the *whole* effort sooner.

When I hear a European saying that "The Americans make speeches at him," or an American that the European "talks in snatches and leaves the point," I think I understand them both, and that the mutual accusation is due to a misunderstanding parallel to the misunderstanding which the General Contrast creates in every other activity. If we admit the Contrast, expect it, make it our first postulate in analysing this very distant world we shall less misjudge; if we ignore it we shall have what are called "rude awakenings."

IV

THE POLITICAL CONTRAST

I. THE CONTRAST IN POLITICAL MACHINERY

Monarchy

THE political machinery of the United States
has derived historically from that of Europe
and in particular from that of eighteenth-century
England.

Many words are common to the two, and the
great mass of constitutional forms has a host of
articles common to both societies. There is even
—far more vigorous than at home—a Party system; that is, the division of a representative assembly, not into spokesmen of conflicting ideas,
but into two teams which adopt such ideas as
their passing watchwords; a system of which it is
the function to test men for government rather
than to ensure the passing of ideas into law.

But these are superficial resemblances in the
shape of the machinery rather than in its essential nature; just as our railway coaches still de-

rive their gauge and much of their form from
the old horse-vehicle, though their method of
action is wholly dissimilar, so does the American
political vehicle resemble the English—and no
more.

The characteristic mark of American political
machinery is not a mere gathering, such as all
men have always normally used; it is not our
English idea of a governing club or clique all
associated, inter-married, and immune—a thing
the American has never heard of; nor even is it
representative assembly which Christendom developed in the Pyrenees at the beginning of the
Middle Ages, but the resurrection in America,
and its rapid growth into what is now a dominant
place, of a certain principle which Europe has
for the moment lost, and without which Europe
remains politically stricken. That principle is
the principle of *executive responsibility vested in
one man:* the principle which must be called, if
we are to be accurate (in spite of false connec-
tions which have gathered around the word), the
principle of *Monarchy.*

The mayoralty of the great American city, the
governorship of the American state, the Presidency of the whole American commonwealth,
these responsible and *individual* offices, vested
each at any one moment in *one* man—these are
the marks of *Monarchy* in action; with its per-

sonal choice of instruments, its personal right
of veto and suspension, its personal power of rec-
ommendation, its personal inflection of policy.

The point is capital, and demands full definition from the outset of its discussion.

All human communities are governed: let
us write that down to begin with. They must
corporately in varying degrees, and they may in
a large degree, affect their own government.
But they are all, in the absolute sense of the
word, *governed*. They are told to do this and
that, and they obey. If they did not do so they
would not be communities at all. Authority
exercised from above is a condition of corporate
existence and unity.

So true is this, that in the very rare moments
when communities openly refuse obedience to
whatever has hitherto governed them, they are
compelled, by the very nature of human society,
to create on the instant some new Orderer in the
place of the old. For a void in command, an in-
terregnum, a nothingness prolonged but for a
few days, would be the ruin of all.

This thing which orders, commands, is obeyed,
has well been called the Prince, to distinguish
it from the Sovereign. The Sovereign is that
which ultimately commands obedience, to which
the ultimate right of command belongs, because

from it, under God, civil authority flows—and that Sovereign is the Community itself.

You can never get away from this truth. And there is no man (of our race at least), from the Greeks to Suarez, who, having thought out these things clearly and dug down to their roots, has not stated this conclusion: the Community is Sovereign. But here let me digress on this essential point: for the misunderstanding of it ruins democracies.

Many of the more intelligent, and therefore traditional, modern men, angered by the antics of the modern state, and having heard that modern state called "democratic," wrangle blindly against the word and denounce all that calls itself democratic; for the sake of that denunciation they denounce democracy even in its most strict definition (which is, a state where the people are the Prince) and they proceed to denounce the obvious truth that, whoever is Prince the Community alone can be Sovereign. They shy and jib at this necessary truth, that the Community is Sovereign. For they say to themselves, "Come . . . ! Surely . . . ! Is not this that horrid thing Democracy? Away with it!"

It is nothing of the sort. The doctrine that the Community is Sovereign is no more democratic than the doctrine that the body needs food is French cooking, or than the doctrine that exchange completes production is Free Trade. The statement that the Community is the ultimate Civil Sovereign, the thing which has ultimate authority in civil affairs, is a mere statement of primary abstract truth common to Monarchy, Democracy, Aristocracy or any mixture of these Princes. In all forms of government the Community is the ultimate lord.

For if the Community be not Sovereign of right, what is?

If William Smith rises up and says, "Behold, I am the Sovereign and all civil authority of right derives from me," what credentials can he show better than those of Abraham Jones or even of Antonio Lemmi? He can show none. He may show plenty of credentials describing him as the better leader or an adviser more cunning than his fellows, or one of those who, from hereditary tradition or other circumstances happens to command awe, and is thence more easily fitted for a ritual position of headship. But he cannot produce credentials of *ultimate* authority. He cannot say, "From my will, from my *person,* emanate the right and the wrong," unless he be the Creator. God only of all Persons can say that. Among men, one man who says it is as much a liar as another.

You will find yourself here met by what the

mathematicians call "a reduction to the absurd."
For if the Community be not Sovereign, but on
the contrary, Alfred be sovereign, then for precisely the same reasons may Hezekiah claim
sovereignty, or Peter. Therefore, ultimate sovereignty is to be discovered in one only, and yet
also in another only—which is a contradiction in
terms and absurd.

If the Community be not Sovereign, what else
is? To that can be no reply but silence.

But, like all fundamental principles, this only
serves us negatively for definition. It only prevents us from making fools of ourselves in statement. It is very valuable because it prevents
gross error, but it is not of immediate detailed
and positive value as a guide to right institutions.
Since the Community is always Sovereign, admittedly, there is an end of it. Whether you like
it or whether you do not, whether you see it
clearly or muddledly or not at all, matters not a
jot. The Community is Sovereign and remains
Sovereign in spite of your like or dislike, your
persuasion or non-persuasion.

It is when we come to the second question,
Who should be the Prince? that you enter the
heat and practice of political debate.

On this question, *"Who is to be the Prince?"*
"Who is to issue the order and expect obedience?" men have wrangled, struck, killed,

argued, persisted, cozened and lied for, it may be, ten thousand years. Nor is the debate settled; nor will it ever be settled finally for mankind.

But we can at least discover a little guidance from the great Greek masters and from our own humble common sense and observation, and we can fix on certain principles underlying the whole debate. And the first principle, which our common sense can discover without the need of a master, is this: *tradition and custom make up the greater part of the Prince.*

The Community is Sovereign, and the moral right to order is from the Community. But the Community cannot, of its nature, leap about capriciously from order to order like an individual. The Community is not static, it is dynamic. It is a living organism acting in time. It comprises men and women of all ages, each derived from other men and women, old or dead, and these in their turn from others. And therefore the Prince, the active agent of the Community, feels custom and is controlled by it. Man being what he is, the formed habit, the traditional thing, is much the major part of the Prince in actual exercise. Very much the most of what we do, under the sense that it must be done, derives from law of this sort; law which is nothing but affirmed and defined Custom. The less conscious we are of this element in the Prince,

the more universally present it is. The permanent habits of thought, of language and of social
convention make up the most of our lives and
are the main Princely Orders which we un-
questioningly obey.

But the social organism being plastic in some
degree, and also not wholly continuous but admitting of movement within itself, there is room
for special or particular law other than Custom,
and for Orders which are consciously received,
often as novelties, and specifically obeyed with a
direct admission of their particular nature. Thus,
it is general social tradition which makes a man
leave his neighbour free to eat or drink what
he can get and choose at his own hours. But in
this there are also special orders always. For
some recognised and defined power in the State
will forbid the use of this and that as food and
drink. It will make special law. Now laws must
be obeyed or society perishes, and laws can only
be made according to some Constitution, that is,
by some Prince. Who or what is that Prince to
be? Who is to make the special laws which all
must obey and (what is more important in practice) to give the *orders,* to command the forces
which compel obedience? To act?

This governing, acting power, the Prince, is
of great moment to us all. His actions are so
direct and immediate, tangible and open to im-

mediate appreciation of praise or blame, they affect us all *Personally* so much, his power over us is so great that on the question who should hold such power has discussion and armed conflict ever raged among men.

The great Greek masters said wisely and finally that this overt Prince could only be one of three kinds; or a mixture of these. He could be one man, or a select body, or all the citizens met together; that is, a *Monarch* or an *Oligarchy* or a *Democracy*.

A new regulation, some direct definable order —for instance, a call to military service—falling upon the individuals of a community and claiming their obedience, must proceed either (1) from one man who is thus held in person responsible for the consequences of the order, and that is *Monarchy;* or (2) it must proceed from some class or college, or council—some body smaller than the State and existing within the State (such as are all assemblies, caucus, chosen, hereditary, or what not), and that is *Oligarchy;* or (3) such an order must proceed from *all* the citizens acting together in universal assembly, and that is *Democracy*.

Those are the three types of Government which may be mixed in any proportions, but which remain distinct in nature and effect.

Wise men, and notably the great Frenchman

Montesquieu (who, being a true creator of ideas, is half forgotten), have here distinguished between three departments in the action of the Prince: These departments are the Legislative, the Executive, and the Judiciary; for all things are trine (an observation upon which you may reflect at your leisure).

The legislative function is that function of the Prince whereby he makes the order. The executive function is that function whereby he executes it; that is, attends to its application, keeps it in vigour, appoints officers to see that it is carried out, and to apprehend and punish those who fail to carry it out. The judiciary function is that in which any subject of the prince, individual or corporate, discovered or pretended by the executive officers to have broken the law, is judged, evidence on his assumed rebellion produced and a decision upon the matter delivered; which decision having been delivered the executive steps in again to accomplish its results; as, the punishment of the delinquent or the setting of him free.

Whether these three powers should be separated or combined is a matter of great importance to determine. For their separation or combination greatly affects the life of the citizens. In modern England to-day, for instance, they are largely combined; the Judge, the Parliamenta-

rian, the Ministers of Government, all form one
body or club. They all act together: judge, politician (or so-called "representative") and Minister of State—or "Crown" are all in league. In
America they are carefully separated. The "representative" is not necessarily (as with us) an
executive minister, nor does he nominate the
magistrates. But all we are concerned with here
is the fact that all three exist in the Prince, in
that overt Prince who acts over his subjects and
is known to them, and is therefore inevitably
responsible to them, and who must be one of
three things, Monarch, Oligarchy, or Democratic
Assembly of all the people, or any of these three
mixed is certain proportions: Monarchy, the
principate of one man (or woman, or child, but
not beast) ; Oligarchy, the principate of an assembly or restricted body of some sort, such as
an elected assembly or an hereditary one; Democracy, the principate of the whole people met in
one place, or at any rate all acting in a direct
fashion together and giving a common order.

In point of fact these three are invariably
mixed in practice. You never get a pure
Monarchy or a pure Oligarchy or a pure
Democracy. Where men have been most wedded
to the idea of monarchy, where the conception
of one man acting as Prince has been so strong
as to clothe that man with the most awful dig-

nity (and even with something of the divine,
making the King into a God), it has been neither
possible nor desired by monarch or people that
assemblies should cease, or that general popular
meeting should cease. Such men have never
governed, and never can govern, without restricted bodies or committees to whom certain
functions are committed. Nor even can they
govern without some way of referring to the
whole people occasionally in one fashion or another, or at least without the whole people
demonstrating their desire in some fashion or
another, if only by mob.

Those who are most wedded to the extreme of
Democracy—as are still, have been for centuries,
and will, please Heaven, for centuries more be,
certain happy mountain valleys of Europe, notably Andorra—cannot keep the people in permanent assembly; even they must have officers
of State.

Those peoples called, loosely, Aristocracies,
that is nations which love to be governed oligarch-
ically by a particular class or assembly, cannot
carry on without *some* admixture of personal
power in their government or without *some* refer-
ence to the people acting as a whole.

The government of the later Roman Empire,
of modern Russia before 1917, was an extreme
Monarchy. Yet in each there was local action

determined by full general assemblies of all the free people upon whom the action fell. (For the unfree are no part of the State.)   Great Britain until quite recently was an extreme example of Oligarchy, or as it is loosely called "Aristocracy" (for Aristocracy should strictly mean government not by a few whom men *like* to be governed by, but by a few whom they are *best* governed by) ; but even so there were relics of popular consultation, and the little group that governed went through the form of having election to assembly for certain of their number by using twisted relics of popular vote.   There was even a trace of Monarchy in aristocratic England; for the ruling class of the eighteenth century in England put up as a puppet king to be the nominal head of the State a foreign fellow from Hanover, much despised as a German boor by the real rulers, the gentry, but allowed a certain nominal status in the machinery of government because he was supposed to give a centre to the State and because the name of King pleased the populace.

There must, then, always be some admixture of the three forms of Prince in any governmental machinery, and the debate does not turn upon which of these forms we shall have so much as upon the *Proportions* in which each should be admitted to rule.   *Proportion* is here, as in all other human matters, from building to making love, the crux of the affair. *Proportion* in the ingredients of Monarchy, Oligarchy, Democracy is what men really debate in their fierce political discussions and armed revolts and usurpations.

For it is vital to the character of the State which of the three elements, the universal gathering, the assembly-clique, the monarch, you shall most emphasise in forming your government; and here I come to the marrow of what I have to say and to the end of this intolerably long digression.

The American people of to-day differ from the Europeans of to-day in this: that they have retained in a very large degree the institution of MONARCHY and are daily increasing its scope. More and more in America do you note the practical power in government of individual men responsible to the people, issuing orders, and seeing that they are obeyed; framing and suggesting policies; vetoing the orders of Assemblies.

The American people owe this immensely important institution to two sources: the foundation of their commonwealth and their own genius presiding over its development. In Europe the institution of Monarchy has progressively declined for a hundred and fifty years, and its decline has brought all manner of evils. But the American Commonwealth and its constituent commonwealths are more and more monarchic, and are thus possessed of something eminently suited to our time and indeed to our blood, while we in Europe lack that something, and are therefore increasingly uneasy under a sense of its loss, and void of direction.

I say that this institution of monarchy has proceeded from the original roots of the American state and states, but also from their genius, that is, their political character, their instinct at work in the formation of their affairs.   This trend to Monarchy is apparent in very numerous forms: the railroad, the factory, finance, the college, but, politically, in three special forms: The Governor of the state, the Mayor of the great city, the President of the whole Federation.

I write here with diffidence, for I am writing of another world.   Only an American can judge whether a foreigner, or rather how much a foreigner, has reached the truth with regard to American affairs.   No foreigner can thoroughly understand them; most foreigners misunderstand them altogether.   But as it seems to me—and I think that here most Americans will agree with me—the political genius of the people has done more in this matter than the original institution. The Governor of the individual State was inherited from the colonial system, but he has become a very different person from what he was

under the colonial system. The Mayor or head-
man of the city is an institution as old as our
race, present everywhere from the lost Mediterranean beginnings of its history thousands of
years ago; yet if there is one institution among
the Americans which has clearly been their own
work it is this institution. For the characteristic
of it is a monarchial government set over immense urban aggregations, such as the earlier
colonial and revolutionary days never dreamed
of. The giving of these great powers to an individual, the making of one man thus responsible, is something that would not have happened
as the great American cities grew up unless it
had been consonant to some civic instinct in the
governed. In Europe it is just the other way:
the larger the city the less the power of the
Mayor. To-day, in spite of a few exceptions
where a committee takes the place of the Mayor,
the Mayoralty is the great distinction between
the American city and the European. Here and
there in Europe the Mayor may, for a moment
(as in the city of Lyons under Herriot, or of
Birmingham under Chamberlain) from personal
character achieve a position faintly resembling
that of the American Mayor. But in the immense majority of cases the Mayor in Europe
does not count. He is a figurehead, and it is an
assembly which really governs the city, and

which, moreover, has in all European countries, but especially in England, far less real power over its own conduct than has an American.

When you come to the institution of the Presidency, although it is a thing deliberately fashioned by the fathers of the country, yet, how greatly has it changed in the five generations between their time and ours!

The written powers are much the same, but the actual powers how vastly increased! There are, I understand, occasional reactions against the successive increase of those actual powers, but the tide continually rises.

Moreover, the conception of the office has changed. It began as a function intended to symbolise national unity and to co-ordinate the action of the separate autonomous States, either for such general purposes as national defence, or on occasions sporadic and unusual, where domestic arrangements common to all the States had to be made and enforced. The conception was far distant from that of an executive immediately affecting all individuals in the Federation.

Further, the choice of the President was left to a college, whose work was originally designed to be one of slow deliberation until they had chosen the worthiest. It has now become what is virtually direct election by the people as a whole.

The American Presidency is to-day far the strongest Monarchy on earth. It exercises authority omnipresent and personally felt by all the citizens. Perhaps its two main functions in the original intention were the maintenance of unity in what was essentially a confederation, and a confederation wherein the lines of cleavage lay between the various states; to which should be added, perhaps, the function of moderator over the general assembly. It has become the very much more powerful, very much more particular, and very much more direct thing which we have before us. What is most characteristic of the change, and most illuminating, this Monarchy has begun to take on the spiritual symbols of power. At the death of Mr. Harding the character of the national mourning, the novel and peculiar depth, emphasis and exaltation of the moment was observed by all. The fusion of the individual with the people—which is the sacramental stamp of Monarchy—was universally present in the general mind.

This large proportion of Monarchy in American political machinery is of the greatest importance in the contrast between the American Republic and the political systems still perilously surviving upon our side of the Atlantic. But it is not only of importance as marking a contrast, it is also, I would repeat (with all the hesitation of one discussing a foreign thing), a good. It may be that I exaggerate that good from a natural reaction which every thinking European feels against the corrupt farce of his own contemptible Parliaments, but a good it does seem to me to be: and I would ascribe more to this increase of Monarchy than to any other factor the stability and security of the American Commonwealth compared with those of Europe.

The prime disadvantage of Monarchy is the opening it gives to caprice; that is, for conflict between the Prince and the Sovereign; conflict between the particular organ which issues special orders, and that whole community in which authority ultimately resides.

The advantages of Monarchy are simplicity and truth. An individual man can be made really responsible, for he has a real will, a body and a soul; an assembly is but an idea. Responsibility in an assembly—a committee or Parliament or Congress is impersonal, and can be shirked the more easily in proportion to the size of the clique of professional politicians (in England about 900). But where a monarch acts the people can judge. Where there is no monarch their judgment may be wasted and often does fall into the void.

Now in the time in which we live the evil of Monarchy is much less of a menace than the good is an obvious advantage; there is far less danger of caprice in the individual governor or of tyranny by him than there is of irresponsibility and corruption in a Congress. Moreover, the limitation of Monarchy by short term, though this makes it none the less a Monarchy, is a check useful in secure times and places. It renders the responsibility most active as referred to the individual, permitting of continual correction, yet maintains the organ unbroken in the structure of the State. Monarchy thus organised perpetually permits the transmission of true general authority from the Sovereign through the Prince. It speaks for, as nothing else can speak for—it *impersonates*—the Community.

I have heard it said by Americans (and it is an excellent example of the way in which either side of the ocean is remote from the realities of the other) that a Prime Minister in modern England has more power than an American President. That most erroneous statement was supported by the citation of powers which the Prime Minister in England is supposed to exercise. A Prime Minister of England is supposed, in theory, to nominate directly all judges, to confer all public honours within the State, to nominate many of the professors in the universities, to decide what legislation shall be presented to Parliament. Parliament having become the degraded thing it is, this seems to mean that the Prime Minister of England is the sole real legislator, for the word "king" is now, unfortunately, with us, used only as a ritual phrase.

Thus we say in England that the Prime Minister "has advised His Majesty" to make some impossible person a Lord, but every schoolboy knows that His Majesty has had nothing to do with it. Now the Prime Minister, during that long and great succession of English gentlemen, which began with Walpole and ended with Mr. Asquith, did have great power. But he was still only the president of a small aristocratic committee, the Cabinet, which itself lay under the ultimate power of a larger aristocratic assembly, the House of Commons. The Prime Minister's power thus subordinated was essentially an aristocratic, not a monarchial power. He was "one of us" among the governing oligarchy.

When, some thirty years ago, England first showed signs of losing her aristocratic tradition, the House of Commons began to lose its character and to fall into public contempt. The cabinets[1] were arranged out of a small club of people

[1] More properly "The Front Benches." It would confuse the text were I to introduce here a digression on the "club" or "clique" method of government, which is the mark of our time at Westminster. But, to put the matter briefly for American readers, the affair stands thus. An existing body of politicians occupying the "Front Benches"

who co-opted new members into their set, and was more and more independent of the failing assembly to which it was nominally subject.

Recently, in the further decline of aristocratic sense this committee-form, or Club-rule, became so degraded that, in its failure, the Prime Ministership *appeared* to acquire an almost irresponsible personal power; but what had *really* happened, as we in England all know, was the breakdown of the Prime Ministership itself. With the decline in power of Parliament and the subsequent decline of the Cabinet, the Prime Minister, left isolated, became the poor servant of financial forces largely international and of the directors of the more vulgar Press. These it was which made and unmade nominal Prime Ministers such as Mr. Lloyd George, and will now continue to make and unmake the unfortunate little men who preserve an appetite for such notoriety as the old political label can give them— but the great function of Prime Minister is dead.

Upon the European continent the modern parliamentary oligarchies, most of them quite recent and all of them exceedingly unpopular,

of the House of Commons, and a corresponding portion in the House of Lords, make a club, out of which alternative cabinets are formed, "Conservative," "Liberal," "Labour," or what not—the terms are mere labels. This club is renewed by co-option among its members, and is not affected by the ruck of lesser politicians outside.

are too young for us to judge what form of real power will eventually overthrow them. But if we take the most vigorous of these experiments, the French, an experiment which has doubtfully survived the Great War, we can perceive how thoroughly the element of Monarchy was eliminated.

The modern and unstable constitution of the French Republic was so framed fifty years ago that the President should have powers almost equivalent to those of a great king. He was to receive vast sums out of the public purse, to maintain high pomp, to choose his ministers as he would, whether within or without the (so-called) "representative" assemblies, to order peace and war, and to be in very truth the head of the armed forces of the community and of the community itself.

But the politicians saw to it that these powers should remain a dead letter; of its characters only one, the basest, the appeal of personal avarice, remained. The French President was sure of accumulating a great fortune rapidly, and without working, out of the taxes. He could save every penny he was paid. The politicians saw to it that all his expenses whatsoever should come out of the public pocket, and that his salary should accumulate, till, at the end of his seven years' term—apart from his opportunities upon

the Stock Exchange—he was certain of millions.
But all this was upon the strict condition that
he did not govern and left the parliamentary oligarchy supreme.

In the absence of Monarchy the French people
have organised themselves spontaneously into
great interests or bodies which preserve, more or
less, the dignity and continuity of the State. The
politicians are still tolerated but less and less
perfectly obeyed. The Universities, the Church,
the great agricultural interests, the industrial
groups, largely look after themselves. And the
judiciary feels and acts much more with the
nation at large than with its unpopular and distressing Parliament. The Army jealously re-
tains great power over its own organisation.
The politicians, indeed, can and do interfere with
the nomination of military chiefs, of magistrates,
and of the higher university positions. They can
and do interfere grievously in matters of religion, and even in the industrial and agricultural
activities of the country. But the interference is
always tentative, against the grain, doubtful and
increasingly weak.

Here is an example. Some years ago financial
forces, working underground, procured from the
politicians—by the usual methods—a special law,
on the model of similar laws already at work in
countries less devoted to personal human dignity

and to the equality of free men in the State.
They procured a law similar to that which we
have in England, whereby the poorer citizens,
earning a weekly wage of less than a certain
amount, should be compelled to register, to carry
on their persons a card identifying them and
marking their movements, and to pay a small,
special, class tax, levied by the employer. The
nominal object was to secure compulsory insur-
ance, but the real object was to keep the work-
man's movements registered under the eye of his
capitalist masters.

Had Monarchy existed in France as it does
in America the law would have been vetoed at
once by the President. It was a gross outrage
repudiated by the whole mass of the nation, and
the people were so angry that a responsible
monarch, whether he were called president or by
any other name, would not have braved that
anger for any sum of money. Well, what happened was this. The French judges, being
largely independent of the politicians, broke that
law by giving decisions which forbade it, in practice, to be executed. They declared it illegal for
any private citizen, however wealthy, to demand
of another, however poor, a return of his wage-
earnings: they declared it illegal for any private
citizen, however wealthy, to levy a tax upon
another citizen, however poor. They affirmed

the equality before the law of every citizen, wage-earning or no.   They thus saved the vigour and the status of the poorer citizens and flouted the Parliamentary oligarchy.

Now it is clearly a very bad state of affairs when the Prince has to be corrected in any commonwealth after such an arbitrary fashion!   Yet haphazard correction in this form or another has become a necessity throughout Europe.   Regular correction of congressional oligarchy by regular organs of the State such as the President with his veto, the Supreme Court with its decisions, fail us in Europe, because the element of Monarchy has been eliminated by our parliamentary politicians, who well know that personal power would be the end of their peculations and petty fame.   In the absence of Monarchy nothing restricts caprice and tyranny in Europe save either the fear of insurrection or action such as that I have just quoted on the part of the French magistrates, whereby some state organ acts outside its due function and saves the situation by what is tantamount to rebellion against the constituted or theoretical public power—against the Prince.

It is true that the extreme of the evil is producing reaction against it.   In France the President is beginning to count.   In Italy Mussolini, with the enthusiastic approval of the Italians,

has kicked the Parliament off its usurped throne.
In Spain the last set of professional politicians
have fled for their lives, in Germany they are
superseded. Popular monarchy must ultimately
return in Europe. But meanwhile Parliamentary oligarchies, with the financiers for their masters, continue to degrade public life in France
and England.

In America Monarchy has no more valuable
function than the function of veto to which I
have just alluded. I have heard it said by
Americans who have spoken to me on this subject that the excellence of a Governor was largely
determined by his judgment and industry in ex-
ercising the veto. With us in Europe the veto
does not exist. When I sat in the House of Commons the discussion was never whether some proposed legislation "put through" by a group of
rich men would be vetoed or not—for there was
no one to veto it—but rather "whether people
would stand it"; some balance of public affairs
was preserved by the ignoble calculation as to
the limits to which corruption could go without
provoking physical resistance.

For Monarchy in Europe we crave. In some
form we *must* restore it. In America it exists
in full force: limited, as it should be limited, but
none the less vital: mixed with the other elements of oligarchical representative assembly

and of direct popular expression as it must always be, but, still, Monarchy; with a vigour of life which we in Europe have, for the moment, lost.

If a test be required it will be found where Americans expect it least. I mean in the contrast between the vigour of resistance to the rule of "Big Business" in America and the absence of resistance to it upon our side of the sea. "Big Business" is essentially monarchial. Single men direct its vast units, productive and financial. Therefore it has a structure far firmer and more incisive than that of any assembly. Therefore it acts with us unrestrainedly over Parliament and is the unquestioned master of the politician. Americans complain of its power in their own commonwealth. Its power there is nothing to its power in ours. Can any one conceive in America such monstrosities as the Marconi affair or the Dope Scandal going unpunished, or the executive permitting the sale of munitions to the enemy in a great war, or a vast revolution in currency being secretly imposed without popular consultation, and, indeed, without the people knowing or being told anything about it? No one can. In America the executive would act. It would be able to act because, against the monarchial power of "Big Business" it has a monarchial power of its own.

I say again that so much praise for conditions which are to-day alien to the European, foreign and very striking to him because they are in such contrast with his own, may be exaggerated. An individual usually does exaggerate the good or evil of any society of which he has but a passing and very brief experience. I have no doubt that Americans, untouched by the evils a lack of Monarchy has brought upon us in Europe, may think their own monarchial element exaggerated, or functioning ill from some other cause than exaggeration. Some may think their monarchic officers, the Mayor, the President, the Governor, too weak; others may think them too strong. Others may deplore the method of choice by huge masses of voters. But it does seem to me that if these Americans had to live under European conditions, not as chance (and usually well-to-do) visitors, but as permanent residents, poor, dependent upon a weekly wage, or upon a small plot of land, if they had to live in Europe as the mass of our people live, they would feel instinctively and perhaps without giving it a name this appetite for Monarchy, this craving for a necessary power which all our people are now feeling—though in them it is still dumb and as yet appears only in the shape of acute ill-ease.

With all forms of government the permanent

and ever-present danger is corruption, that is, the preference by public men of their own interests to the public interests. As a remedy for this permanent and ever-present peril of society, Monarchy acting with and limited by occasional direct appeal to the people, armed or voting, and aided by local democratic institutions, is the only remedy mankind has discovered—with one exception: and that one exception is Aristocracy.

It *is* true that when a community desires to be governed by one special class acting through an assembly chosen from its body, when it reveres that class and gives it a sort of religious sanction, the state is strong and well ordered: and such a state we call *Aristocratic*. Especially is such a state strong and well ordered in its conduct of foreign affairs, and in its immunity from civil strife. Venice, Carthage, England during all her modern greatness, were aristocratic states; and they were marked by this continuity of success abroad and of peace within: so much so that the great tutor of our race, Aristotle, presented the Constitution of Carthage at its close as the best he knew. But the Aristocratic State is not to be had at will. It proceeds from a certain character in the citizens, local and peculiar nor generally discovered in the run of communities. It is a rare phenomenon. It cannot be proposed as a model which any state may adopt, any more than a genius for this or that art can be proposed as a model for any man at random.

There is also this tragic foredoom brooding over aristocratic states, that they cannot renew themselves: when the temper of reverence for a special class declines, they fail. And when they fail they fail for ever.

But they have a long run for their money.

II.   THE CONTRAST IN POLITICAL SPIRIT.

I. *The American Activity of Corporate Will.*
II. *The American Worship of the Constitution.*

A contrast in the machinery of government is one thing. A contrast in the general political spirit between two civilisations is another. The former is largely the product of the latter, and I should, perhaps, have logically taken it first. But I took the contrast in political machinery before the contrast in political spirit because I thought the concrete example, familiar to everybody, was the better introduction; and also because, although the facts of American Government are well known in Europe, the lesson to be drawn from those facts—the lesson of Monarchy—was ignored. Moreover, the matter was of especial interest to me as a European; much

more than to any American readers I may have
the honour to reach. We in Europe are—in the
great nations—sick and pining for *Monarchy,*
that is, for responsibility in Government. In
the lack of it our societies are failing, just as the
body fails through lack of some vital element in
its nutrition. In America that institution is
vigorous and informs all government.

Such is the contrast in political machinery:
the contrast in the political spirit between the
Old World and the New is, of course, a larger
thing. However strong as a preservative the
American institution of Monarchy, in its three
forms, may have proved, it would not have func-
tioned as it has and does but for some political
spirit behind it.

Now the mark of the American political
spirit as opposed to the European is the mixture
of two things: *First,* the *permanent* activity of
corporate opinion and will; *secondly,* the worship of a Constitution.

I will deal with these in their order, and first
discuss the *permanent* American activity of corporate will: the way in which Americans keep
an uninterrupted observation of government.

I. *The American Activity of Corporate Will.*

Modern men, in Europe as in America, pro-
claim to weariness the title of *Democracy:* most

men as adherents, some very powerful thinkers as opponents of it. And this title is used, not, of course, of the form of government properly called Democracy (which is government by the whole people met in assembly), but for I know not what vague though brilliant vision of "elbow room" or freedom from wanton interference by others, coupled with an insistence upon equality with any one who may pretend to be the superior of the speaker in any capacity, let alone in general.

This modern talk is loose and badly worded, but the idea behind the talk is soundly based upon two instincts in man which it is very necessary to satisfy if man is to be happy. It is based upon man's instinct for action as an individual, ever driving him to create and to be; and it is based upon man's corresponding instinct of individual honour which very justly represents the arrogance of one proclaiming himself the superior of his companions.

But when you have said that about this air of "Democracy" you have said pretty well all there is to say about it.

The great majority which to-day revels in the vague idea and proclaims it for a good, enjoy in doing so a sense of fullness and of rough dignity—both very pleasant things.

Those who criticise, deny, or oppose the

modern talk of "Democracy" are principally
occupied, if you look closely at their argument,
in throwing into relief those necessary qualifications without which the vague ideas of equality
and freedom fails to satisfy men: make men
not more but less happy. For instance, they
emphasise the human need for attachment to a
leader through certain qualities (*e.g.* his superior skill in ordering, or his superior foresight).
To recognise *specific* superiority in another is
a good and joyful thing. Man loves service,
especially the service of the worthy; and loyalty
is a personal emotion highly blessing its possessor.
Again, they remind their opponents that you
cannot have freedom without order—this is one
of those obvious statements which can be made
with the least effort and are therefore exceedingly common.

Again, these critics of "Democratic" talk say
that man's creative effort runs to waste if it be
not canalised, and they therefore emphasise the
good of strong command in a community, saying, "You work better under an external power
than at random, and your work is more satisfac-
tory to you when it is thus framed."

Now my point in what follows is, that this
loose modern talk of "Democracy" does *not* distinguish American from European life: Americans are not more given to it than Europeans.

The contrast in political spirit between America and Europe lies not in the desire for freedom to act by choice, nor in the desire for personal dignity—all men feel these—but in their attempted maintenance in Europe through the tradition or stuff of the State, in America through conscious and *permanent* corporate action.

In the United States, for causes some of which are apparent, but most of which are mysterious, the expression of corporate opinion, its presence, its drive are *permanent*. In Europe they are sporadic. Corporate political action is with them like daily life; with us it is like battle.

I have said that some of the causes of this are apparent, and the most obvious is the fluidity of American Society.

This is due, in part, to the unceasing stream of new arrivals which marked that community for nearly a century between the end of the Napoleonic Wars and the Great War of 1914. But it is also due to the nature of American physical expansion. Even if there had not been this perpetual stirring of the waters by the incoming stream, there would have been, and there was, the steady westward-setting tide of native movement, very rapid (by our European standards), and accelerated by the coming of the railway in the nineteenth century. It was inevitable

with a people who had before them days' and
weeks' journeys of fertile land to be occupied,
a boundless field.   It still remains boundless,
awaiting human energy to exploit it: for though
it fills with men, a vast store of force lies there
open to new uses.

Nor is this all.   There was a third factor,
which was the rooted habit of come and go.
There was not only the steady western tide, not
only the pouring influx, there was also a social
tradition, early established and confirmed, of
moving at will and frequently in every direction.
If you were to make a statistic at the present
day, three hundred years after the first plough
broke the soil of the northern continent, a statistic showing what men made what journeys in a
year: what men died in a State other than the
State of their birth; in a township other than the
township of their birth; a statistic of the movements of a particular man during his life-time
from place to place; a statistic of the points in
which the various members of one generation of a
family were born; a statistic of the points where
each established his centre of activity after reach-
ing manhood—if you were to combine all these
and make a general statement, you would have
such a picture of internal mobility within the
unit of the American Republic as no other commonwealth has come near to showing (not even

the nomads of Asia, still less any settled populace of the Old World) in all recorded history.

But, I repeat, such visible causes are not the main causes of the thing. The American habit of common political action, unceasingly maintained, springs mainly, as do all other of the social phenomena, from forces which we cannot seize, which proceed from the very air and the spirit of the soil, and from compulsions still deeper which urge, each in its region, the souls of men.

At any rate, the phenomenon is there; the corporate opinion of the United States in any matter, the opinion of a city, of a village, of a whole state, of a religious group, of an industrial group, of the agricultural interest, of the mass of the people as one unit—is unceasingly active and at work. It exercises a strict control over all that is done by assemblies and the more powerful personal governors. It does much more by spreading a universal atmosphere upon this point or that, making the citizens take for granted this or that as the expressed and unquestioned spirit of their fellows at the moment upon some public question. In a word, initiative, in America, is with the crowd. Initiative in Europe is not with the crowd, save in special moments when the crowd acts exceptionally and under some urgent necessity. The French Republican calls it "Coming down into the Street"—a special action; but the American lives there. The English Liberal leaves government to his betters. The American acknowledges none.

Take, for instance, the discussions on what is called Prohibition. Very varied and conflicting arguments and desires are expressed by Americans upon that new policy. It is everywhere discussed, supported, opposed, as would any such great change be in any country. But the method, the air, of the debate is not at all what it would be with us. With us its opponents or supporters would not refer to an inviolable standard of public decision, nor would their conflict be close and continual. In America both factors are omnipresent. It is a "Constitutional Amendment," and therefore very difficult to remove. It is to be attacked by the legislatures of separate States introducing difficulties to its administration—or supported by them. It is defeated in private life by reliance on special legal actions—for instance, the refusal in many states to allow search without a warrant.[1] And

[1] With us in England the name and faint memory of "The Warrant" still survive; but in practice this check to unlimited executive action no longer exists. A policeman goes into any man's house at will and looks into any matter he chooses to. Not only has liberty thus disappeared as against the State Official, but a similar invasion of private life is exercised by the hired servants of wealthy societies. Any man in uniform can do what he

meanwhile the play of public opinion on either
side is direct, unceasing and closely locked, while
there is unanimity on one point—the abolition
of the Saloon or public drinking-place devoted
to drinking alone and the drinking of spirits at
that. It is certain that the Saloon is abolished—
not because an act of authority abolished it, but
because a public opinion—I do not say a majority—organised and active, supports that act. It
is certain that any modification of the law will
come, if it comes, by the play of ceaseless public
discussion and its effect on the highly complicated machinery of voting.

It is certain that in America no small wealthy
minority could impose its will as the brewing
and distilling millionaires have imposed theirs
upon England. Their "Temperance" policy,
reducing their labour bill by restricting hours
of sale while leaving the *amount* unrestricted, has
vastly increased their dividends—as it was intended to do.

Now supposing Prohibition to be imposed
upon a European community. There would, of
course, be an element of popular will in the
matter, for it would be impossible to make so
vast a change by an act of mere tyranny. But

will, in a poor man's house at any rate, in the name of
the League for this, that and the other—or even of a
railway company.

I affirm that in any European community—
even in the small Scandinavian countries, which
are the nearest parallel in this particular matter
of Prohibition—you would not have this active
discussion and this active concensus upon the
methods of offence and attack, still less this
active concensus upon one point which you have
in America: the abolition of the Saloon.   In
the larger European states a law thus imposed
would be shaken off when or if it became intolerable, not before.   It would then be shaken
off certainly by a corporate act, though probably
the final effort would be that of a minority.
But the action would be spasmodic. *And unless
and until such sudden popular upheaval took
place nothing would be done.*

Here is another example of what I mean.
All representative assemblies if they are not
aristocratic are corrupt.   That may be postulated
as a general truth in political science.   It is an
inevitable consequence following upon the very
nature of the institution.   Give power of the
purse to a number of random individuals in-
spired by no special class code of honour and
checked by no special necessities of class presentation, nor moved to observe some special
dignity through the worship directed towards
them by their fellow-citizens, and they will as
a matter of course pick the public pocket.   They

will naturally and always prefer their private
interests to those of the State, save in such
great crises as call forth fear and shame even in
politicians.   A representative of the common
sort chosen from a crowd mechanically, the professional politician as the type is most accurately
and justly called to-day in England, will, in
normal times, fill his pockets at the public expense, and, indeed, does so in all countries with
regularity and precision.   "After all" (says he
to himself), "the community is so rich!   And I
must live   .   .   .   and it does no very great
harm   .   .   .   and everybody else does it all
around me."   The corruption is usually petty,
but on the part of specially skilful, cunning and
unscrupulous politicians is sometimes enormous.
But on a large scale or a small corruption is as
universally attached to our non-aristocratic
European parliaments as fleas are to dogs.   We
expect it; and our expectation is not disappointed.

But observe how very differently this disease
is treated in the United States and in Europe!
In Europe we deal with it by occasional up-
heavals.   We deal with it more or less drastically
in different countries.   In some it is allowed to
go to great lengths and to run for years.   The
exposure and even punishment of what are called
"parliamentary scandals" never take place at

shorter intervals than, say, five or ten years, and
the action is always sporadic and jerky and unnatural.[1] It is a sort of check or protest. Now
and then it culminates in something revolutionary as recently in Italy, when men will stand no
more of it, and sweep it away by the appoint-
ment of a dictator or by a radical reform in the
personnel and means of choice of the assembly.

But in the United States the public watch
over politicians is permanent. It is not an exaggeration to say that every day, even if you are
travelling over a comparatively limited area,
your newspaper deals with one or another example of corruption in an elected person, exposes it and denounces it.

That this is a healthy sign all will admit, except, perhaps, people of that intellectual level
which regards the recognition of evil as worse
than evil itself. To say that this ceaseless play
of exposure is a mark of greater corruption in
America than is to be found in the Old World
is nonsense. No one with a knowledge of the
House of Commons or the French Chamber of

---

[1] We had an excellent example the other day in England.
The politicians had for some years sold peerages to men
more and more grotesque. After each new sale there was
a clamour of impotent protest, and the thing went on. At
last a South African millionaire of the most startling type
broke the Camel's Back. The House of Lords itself began
to tell truths openly, and the purchasing millionaire fled, as
did the vendors of the title.

Deputies, or of their now happily suppressed Italian brethren, would dream of saying that American public life was more corrupt than European. The difference lies not in the presence of the disease, which is universal, but in the method of treating it; and here the difference is astonishing. Corruption with us in Europe is essentially private. It is like the actions of a man in his own room. That privacy is subject to occasional interruption: the Deputy or Member of Parliament is sometimes exposed in the midst of his thieving; but the interference is always met by indignant remonstrance, and his colleagues exclaim in chorus against the bad taste of those who would thus inspect the sacred domesticity of Parliament. Corresponding action in the United States is not private. The politician who peculates does so under a grave and *constant* risk, a risk which he always feels and for which he has to be prepared. That is because the corporate will is always awake and because the man who exposes corruption is, in America, heartily applauded and supported by his fellow-citizens.

I have been told by many Americans (and naturally by all my acquaintances engaged in European professional politics) that this ceaseless exposure and purging of an evil has two great evils attached to it which outweigh its good. Indeed, our politicians in Europe not only take it for granted that the evils outweigh the good, but do not admit any advantage at all in the practice of examining and exposing knavery in public life.

These evils are (1) the certificate that in the general process innocent men will be suspected and (2) the production, by such perpetual exposure, of a sort of atmosphere or consciousness of political weakness. If the mass of people (it is said) get to believe that their representatives are corrupt the security of the State is weakened.

I admit the evils, but I do not for a moment admit that they outweigh the good. If an innocent man is accused he must take the rough with the smooth. He has deliberately entered professional politics. He knows his trade to be tainted, he must run the risk. A man does not go in for professional politics without some idea of advantage to himself. He desires to be talked about or to have power, even if he does not desire to purloin public money. He cannot see what goes on around him as a member of these little political oligarchies without either denouncing their corruption or winking at it. If he denounces it he cannot long remain a member of the assembly he thus betrays. If he winks at it he is a partner in the guilt of his fellows.

I noticed when I sat in the House of Com-

mons that the more honest members were especially indignant at any imputation against *their*
honour: and whenever one of our regularly re-
current public scandals broke out their friends
were eager to profess that *these* men, at any rate,
were exceptions to the general rule. But the
reason of this excitability and of those eager pro-
tests was that they had sat among, and tolerated
in others, the things of which they were unjustly
accused. I say that men who associate with and
tolerate the corruption of their fellows are in an
absurd position when they protest their private
innocence of a public evil which they have
shamefully condoned. They must have known
its effect upon the State. It was their duty as
patriots to prevent it and to punish it.

Further, I do not admit that perpetual exposure of representative corruption, though it does
create a general consciousness of weakness in
the State, causes thereby an evil greater than
the good which it does. The recognition of evil
is healthy. Representative assemblies are and
most always will be corrupt. To say that and
yet to support their continuance is tantamount
to saying, "I think this institution necessary.
But I see that it carries with it an attendant evil.
I will not shut my eyes to that evil, I will regard
it as permanently present, I will restrain it as
best I may." That, as it seems to me, is the right

attitude to take towards all necessary evils in this world, and therefore I conclude that the attitude taken by Americans towards their assemblies is sound. The Americans expect representative bodies (in large communities) to be corrupt— nor are they disappointed in their expectation. But they do not think that representative assemblies can be, or should be, eliminated on that account. They think such assemblies should be constantly watched and their vices continually corrected by exposure; and in this process the American people exercise a *constant,* a *permanent,* control over their servants, whereas in Europe such control is at the best spasmodic and capricious.

That is the first great mark in the contrast between the American political spirit and our own.

The second is the *Worship of the Constitution.* To this I will now turn.

II. *The American Worship of the Constitution.*

It is the mark of long-established societies, shaped in tradition, that they extend the religious instinct to include their institutions. All the states of antiquity reposed upon such a practice and instinctively made of it their principle of continuity and of survival. Mediæval and more recent Christian societies acted in the same fash-

ion. The French before the Revolution had for
the Capetian Monarchy just that religious awe
which is felt for a national shrine or sacrificial
rite. The whole of the West in the later Dark
Ages and early Middle Ages had the same awe
for the hierarchic bonds of society: the bond of
feudal loyalty in temporal matters, the bond of
official subordination leading up to the Papacy
in spiritual matters.

Modern Europe has, from a series of acci-
dents, lost this cement. It has crumbled away.
The various institutions familiar to men are each
examined sceptically, each asked to give a reason
for its existence, and therefore each undermined:
and this is particularly true of the *governmental*
institutions of the various countries into which
our age-long occidental culture is now divided.

It is remarkable that in the United States this
ancient, profound and preservative instinct has
revived to an intense life, and has attached itself to one central institution not yet a century
and a half old: *The Constitution.*

We have here the converse, the necessary sup-
plement, to that permanent, unceasing watch
and correction which corporate opinion and will
in the United States sets over public servants.
Deprived of such a check as this worship of the
Constitution, the action of ceaseless criticism and
correction would be disruptive. Provided with

this check, a continual discussion of public affairs, a continual denunciation of dishonesty in public servants, does not breed instability.

The Constitution of the United States has two main characters, one of method, the other of regulation. That of method is the provision of obstacles to change, that of regulation is the Supreme Court.

The Constitution of the United States, as framed by the founders of that Commonwealth, can suffer no change, however minute, save by the approval of each legislature within the Federation, and that approval accepted by a large, not a bare, minority. The change once effected, however vast, remains unalterable unless or until it can be reversed by a similar process. Meanwhile, the capital institution of the whole Commonwealth, the Supreme Court (a small bench of judges whom the President appoints for life), decides in any particular case what the Constitution does and does not enjoin.

These two characters are peculiar to the society which they govern. There is nothing like them elsewhere on earth; but they could have no practical meaning save for the absolute quality of the respect they command. Commanding as they do that absolute respect, that religious awe, which forbids any question of their authority, they are wholly conservative of the

Commonwealth. Let this principle of sanctity applied to the Constitution suffer sceptical encroachment, let this religion be weakened by a shifting of its authority to an attempted rational basis, and the American Commonwealth will dissolve.

The non-rational, transcendental cult of the Constitution is a political Principle of Life for the Americans. *Sine Auctoritate Nulla Vita.*

There is something arresting and majestic in this spectacle of a new structure, framed deliberately in the full light of modern record and contemporary with men whom our fathers knew, achieving that sacramental, intangible air of immemorial things. Here is a something which has not grown, but was planned; which took no force from the weight of centuries, but was put together, mechanically, in a few years; which had no foundation in sanctifying legend and the appeal to some vastly distant heroic time, but reposed on the known debates, arguments and votes of recent men. Yet it acts with exactly that *kind* of authority which distinguished the half-divine kingships of old.

A profound instinct moves the American people to that political religion, to this necessary guarantee of unity and permanence; nor is anyone competent to examine, let alone to criticise, the American Commonwealth who does not grasp the weight and value of that instinct, and who fails to appreciate its function. The worship, not the rational acceptation, of the Constitution is the bed-rock upon which all that political world stands; and an enemy who would disintegrate the American people must first begin by exciting enquiry, and therefore doubt, upon the claims of that emotion.

The matter—so surprising to the modern European, so unusual to him and remote from his experience—can be conveyed by a parallel.

If a law imposed upon one of our European societies is odious to a great number of citizens it is at once evaded and frustrated. If it be, or become, odious to that society as a whole it falls into desuetude or is formally repealed. *If its maintenance is still enforced by some one organ of the State that organ will be broken.* Indeed, the only check we have left in Europe against tyranny exercised by finance through Parliaments is the dread of a popular action which could *destroy* the organ—Parliament—if it went too far in oppression.

If such a law appear in the United States it is subject to the same processes of opposition and to the same solvents of desuetude, etc. *But its maintenance being enforced by the organ of the Constitution, there is never a question of break-*

ing that organ. Any inconvenience (one might say), almost any grievance, would be left un-remedied rather than recourse should be had to attack upon the ultimate and supreme authority in public life.

This loyalty is a factor of strength incalculably great. The instinct defending it is an instinct comparable to that of the Germans for their racial culture, of the French for arms, of the English for the sea.

Attached to this devotion we observe what seems to too many Europeans the paradox of American respect for law. The process of law is perpetually over-ridden in matters of high importance—for instance, in the trial of a man on a grave charge. A body of partisans seize the prisoner upon occasion and deal with him as they will, often to the death. Sporadic violence is familiar. Claims are defended by individual force. Yet, side by side with this, you may note the most surprising minuteness of respect paid to some regulations affecting a half-deserted countryside, a vast space in which the mere me-chanical action of a police would be impossible, and where the carrying out of a law—apparently insignificant—clearly depends upon the respect paid to it by men too scattered to be coerced and even accustomed to private feud. Why is this?

Both phenomena, the irregular and the regular action, spring from the same root; but the second is by far the more remarkable. The irregular action is the fruit of a looseness in social structure inseparable from an unprecedentedly large and rapid expansion over vast spaces and from a ceaseless foreign influx. The observance of law (and that in surprising detail), when it cannot be enforced, is the fruit of this same looseness of structure, *in which the individual feels a menace to society and therefore to himself if law fails*. It is the effect of a conclusion, more or less conscious, to which each man has come that in the absence of material force to uphold what was everywhere, and is still in a large part of the territory, a *scattered* society, only individual and voluntary co-operation can uphold it.

I repeat, of the two American phenomena, lawlessness and adoration of law, the latter is far the more remarkable. A man of doubtful morals respecting a lonely letter box in a desert state, a lazy man mending his allotted piece of road on a mountain trail, impress me far more than a lynching or a shooting affray in the same county. These you may hear of in any place where distance and perpetual movement make order difficult to maintain. They are a natural concomitant of such conditions. But the spontaneous support of things necessary to the com-

mon life is a less explicable thing: and most
admirable.

*   *   *   *   *

I would sum up, then, the Political Contrast
between American society and our own thus:—

(I.) As regards Political Machinery, the mark
of America is the Recovery of Monarchy, that
is, the responsibility of one man for the execution of laws, the maintenance of function, the
direction of effort. The Rule of One Man in the
economic units of society, in its educational units,
in the city, the particular state, and over the
whole commonwealth.

(II.) As regards the Political Spirit underlying this Machinery, I discover a *constant* and
regular action of the corporate will and of public supervision which, with us in Europe, is
sporadic and occasional only (in Aristocratic
England all but unknown), and this action is
contained and regulated by a religious attitude
towards those fundamental institutions which
give unity to the State.

V

THE AMERICAN MILITARY EXPERIENCE

NO European can understand the American people who does not appreciate the effect upon them of their military past; nor can any American understand Europe unless he understands the very different effects which their very different military pasts have had upon the chief European communities.

Victory or defeat, invasion, its successful repulsion or shameful acceptance, the presence or absence of great loss in human lives, the presence or absence of loot and ravishing, the exaltation of victory and the bitterness of defeat, knowledge or ignorance of civil war—these things have a profound effect upon the soul of a nation. For my part I regard them as coming next to religion in their power to mould a people's inmost self. Contrary to the modern fashion, I put the military experience of a nation far above its economic method in scale of those forces which create a commonwealth.

Now the American people differ from all European peoples in their military experience; but if you will examine that experience, you will discover they come nearest to the French, and are farthest from the English in this matter.

This sentence will be unintelligible to many of my readers, and needs, therefore, a full development by way of apology; I believe it to be true. The parallel of American military experience with French is remote, but the contrast with the English is immediate and undeniable.

The military experience of the American Commonwealth has three main chapters: The first chapter is the prolonged resistance to, and advance against, the pressure of savagery. The second is the foundation of a nation in victory, a *land* victory in American eyes, for it was one in which that nation made little *of its own craft* upon the sea. The third chapter is the great Civil War, wherein that nation again confirmed its unity. The last two of these bring in that parallel with France which I have mentioned, and all three furnish a high contrast with the corresponding experience of the English.

With the Americans of the War of Independence, as was the case of France in her revolutionary and Napoleonic wars, an ardent and determined minority achieved success and created a new State, carrying with it the sluggish, in-

different majority and a hostile minority upon
the other wing. As in the case of France (though
in a fashion shorter, sharper and more decisive)
civil war was made familiar to that new State
before a stable equilibrium could be reached. In
those two points you have the parallel which
makes so many Americans—the bulk of them, I
think—secretly sympathetic with the French
military temper. Each of the two nations has
had those tragic but also exalted experiences
which profoundly affect the national soul.

Now the military tradition of Great Britain is
utterly different. Great Britain has enjoyed—
for so long a time that all memory of inheritance
to the contrary has disappeared—a profound
domestic peace. Great Britain became with the
Reformation, and remained, an aristocratic society, which only in our own time has begun to
turn into a plutocracy. This aristocratic structure bred in Englishmen a passionate and *united*
patriotism, which is the chief and the best fruit
of aristocracy. This State enjoyed an increasing
security which, after Waterloo, became a thing
taken for granted like a function of Nature itself. This Security—the great mark of the English, and the source of half their humour, im-
perturbability and pride—was due to a supreme
mastery in the art of seamanship. How much
the English are seamen is a commonplace, and

how much the command of the sea has made England is also a commonplace; but what is not a commonplace, unfortunately, is knowledge of the details which still prove this English temper. Go where you will throughout the world, an English ship is better managed than the ship of any other nation. The tradition of the sea seems, with the English, to be in another class from the same tradition in any other people—even the Scandinavians.

There is, in truth, an alliance between the English and the sea which no other nation knows. It has survived the great economic revolution which has by this time cut off the mass of the English people from their own origins and turned them into the townsmen of the industrial towns. This supremacy at sea—which was a moral more than a material supremacy—has been the great military experience of the English. Relying upon this, the English have used only small professional armies; relying upon this, they quite forgot (and are still most reluctant to admit) the principle of a universal national levy; favoured by this complete security of defence, the English became both ignorant of and contemptuous of defeat or even peril. Their small professional armies were excellent; they could be landed wherever maritime supremacy chose to use them. When they were outnumbered or

outmanœuvred they could always retreat to the
sea or fortify themselves upon a port; they could
await the opportunity for victory and strike at
their own moment, coming in at the end triumph-
antly as the invaluable unexhausted allies of much
greater continental forces.

In this way there was built up round the English mind a military experience of unquestioned
universal, continuous success, coupled with a general ignorance of what was meant by land warfare upon a large scale, and a vast and most
legitimate pride in that wherein it had no rival,
the handling of boats.

There is here a complete contrast to the military experiences which have affected the Americans. To the American citizen conscription—
"the draft," as he calls it—is a known and familiar
expedient. To the American citizen the necessity
of enforcing by arms on land a political contention is the very essential of his history. To the
American citizen the great losses, risks, and triumphs of war, and of war by land upon a great
scale covering vast distances and using millions
of men, have long formed an essential part of the
national being.

Having said so much, it is important to qualify;
to insist upon one character at least in which the
American military experience is differentiated—
not only from that of England but from that of

all Europe. I do not allude to that original experience of a continued struggle with barbarism
which is peculiar to American history and has
been of powerful effect in the forming of American character; I mean in this unique combination: *a continuously pacific intent with occasional and sporadic universal military efforts.*

With us in Europe it is not so; nations are
either more or less permanently military or
more or less permanently pacific; and it is their
geographical circumstance, coupled with their
internal constitution, which makes them one or
the other. Many a people in the course of European history would have demanded nothing better, after a bout of successful warfare, than to
forget arms altogether and to settle down to their
own enrichment; but the high differentiation of
Europe has always forbidden that, and there is
in Europe only one state, the English, which has
been permanently removed from the military
necessity and temper. Thus we have in Europe
to-day before our eyes a paradoxical situation
of communities which have to be prevented *by
force* from adopting universal military services,
and the conquered peoples, such as the Magyars
and the various German States, are compelled by
their victors to the maintenance of small professional armies alone.

Of all Europe it is only England which voluntarily (and enthusiastically) abandons universal service.

But in the case of the Americans you have a very odd mixture of two things, which in Europe cannot be found together: at least, I call it odd, because to us Europeans it is strange and un-experienced. There is, I have said, the back-ground of a continuous pacific intent, and the more or less conscious knowledge that at a mo-ment's notice a military effort may have to be made. The American mind has none of that con-temptuous repose in security which was the mark of the English mind until the Great War, and which still largely colours (to the grave peril of England) most of English political thought. No American would be surprised if some prophet could reveal to him a further civil struggle in the future; but, on the other hand, a further civil struggle in the future, or even the necessity of defence against aggression from abroad, is not a threat immediate or continuous, and therefore the military condition of permanent armament is absent. Not only is it absent, but it always appears to the American something unnatural, and something connected in an obscure way which baffles him with what he would call "milita-rism." I have spoken to very many men in America upon this subject, and I find that nearly all of them regarded the German army in the

Prussian Germany between 1870 and 1914, and even the French and Polish and Italian armies to-day, as luxuries, and evil luxuries at that. The condition of permanent armament is alien to the American mind, because the conditions under which permanent armament arises and seems necessary to a people have not yet, and perhaps never will, affect the American Commonwealth.

I should not leave this short chapter upon a very important factor in the making of a nation without alluding to that small but most significant detail, the American study of war, the interest of American scholars in the art of war.

The American monographs upon war, not only mediæval and ancient but modern, are as good as any work of the kind now being done in the world; and the truly military temper of the Americans is here admirably illustrated.

These are two pre-eminent tests which should always be applied to work of this kind, the one moral, the other mathematical. In order to judge the degree in which military history and analysis should be admired, we must measure for ourselves: (1) The degree of political detachment in the writer, and (2) The degree of common sense in his synthesis. The moment you get the element of boasting, the introduction of unnecessary emotion, the abandonment of "the game of chess" feeling in military writing, there is a danger-signal. Not all jingo or boastful military work is bad; but the jingo element in military work is an index of the unmilitary mind. Now that element is singularly absent from American work. It is very far from absent in American newspaper and political discussion of war; but in the strictly military studies which have Americans for their authors, in the lectures delivered in the military colleges, in the monographs proceeding from American pens upon battles and campaigns in the past, the absence of this detestable and puerile defect is most noticeable. "Write of battle," said one great authority upon our side of the water, "so that no one can tell whether you desire victory for the one side or the other, or are indifferent to both."

Well, if that be a canon, American work observes it admirably, and the second rule is also well observed. Most worthless is any military writing which piles detail on detail and shows the most perfect knowledge of instruments and ground if, in the synthesis built up from so much examining, in the integration of so many differentials, common sense be absent.

How silly it is, for instance, to gibe at old Blücher for the delay in coming up in flank at Waterloo; no matter what the mass of detailed knowledge with which you back up your gibe, if you have not the common sense to see that the

Fourth Prussian Army Corps was *compelled* to go through Wavre and to cause that congestion which in its turn produced the delay, it is mere lack of common sense which attributes to a General of Blücher's capacity an elemental blunder in the ordering of the advance. I happen to know why the Fourth Corps was compelled to go through Wavre. For whilst I was examining that terrain closely in the year 1913 I discovered a little bluff above the river, too low to appear in any map, but just too high for guns to negotiate: to this bluff we owe the inability of the Fourth Corps to cross up-stream. Even if I did not know the reason, I should suspect the writing of a man who accounted for Blücher's delay by nothing more than slackness or stupidity; I should say that such an interpretation lacked common sense. Now this saving element of common sense I have found in the greater part of American military work.

The presence of these two qualities in American military writing is to me a sufficient proof of the way in which the historical experience of the nation has formed a just tradition.

It may be that the great change in modern war will render all this academic, and that the military character of the Americans will change; but the primal impulse given them by their wide and profound military experience during the first century and a half of their existence as an independent nation cannot be eliminated. As I have said, their institutions, their young commonwealth was founded in victory over the foreigner and was confirmed by victory in civil war. Such national memories are an endless source of strength. They forbid the illusions of security and superiority which are the subtle poisons of nations long defenced from attack and ignorant of war on their own soil, steeped in the false and weakening tradition of an unbroken domestic peace.

VI

THE RELIGIOUS CONTRAST

I COME to the Contrast in Religion between the New World and the Old. It is much the most difficult point to emphasise, and that for three reasons.

First, that modern men have forgotten the social effect of religion, ascribing to almost any other cause, economic or physical, what is in truth the result of men's doctrines.

Secondly, that modern men hold doctrines without defining them, therefore without knowing they hold them.

Thirdly, that, after language, the one point in which a false similarity most masks the essential difference between America and England is the point of religion.

Religion is at the root of all culture, and societies differ more from difference in religion than from difference in any other factor. It is more powerful than race, far more powerful than physical environment. If anyone doubts this, let him consider the example of Islam.

One culture covering such races as Negroes on the one hand, Berbers—who in feature are indistinguishable from Europeans—on the other hand (and every sort of type intermediary between, or external to, these) cuts off a whole section of humanity from the rest of the race and stamps it with a particular mark never to be mistaken.

Now, as I have said, in religion the United States would seem to offer less contrast to Europe, and especially to England, than in any other social factor, with the exception of language. They form part of the general culture of Christendom, but they have also in particular the same essential of varying, independent, Protestant religious bodies which are the special mark of England. In the United States, as in England, you find great Baptist, Congregational, Presbyterian, Methodist, and other communities; you find the small, wealthy, highly-cultured Unitarian body centred there in Pennsylvania as you find it centred upon Birmingham and the Midlands in England. You find what is essentially the same communion as the Church of England under the title of Episcopalian; a similar congeries is not to be found in any European country beside England.

The similarity is striking, and might be thought conclusive against the thesis I have maintained in this book. For while we know that similarity in language has no necessary correspondence to similarity in social structure and spirit, with religion it is powerfully otherwise; and a similar religious system should, it would seem, produce a similar society.

And so it would, were that similarity exact: but, as in the case of language, it acts rather as a mask for what is at the root a profound, increasing and operative contrast which is driving the two worlds apart. And the contrast lies in these two things: *First*, that the balance of religious communities is very different in one case from what it is in the other. *Secondly*, that America stands apart from the interactions of European thought.

These two characteristics in the religious situation of the New World develop a continually widening divergence from that of the Old, and are overshadowed, like everything making up American society, by that mysterious but undeniable and potent influence which is the Genius of the Place, and which gives it, in our European eyes, a wholly foreign tone.

The balance of various religious bodies is the first point of difference I have noted, and it is capital. By the proportion of the ingredients it is that bodies in the physical world differ. The same ultimate constituents combined in one fashion produce coal, and in another the diamond: in the one case the Roman cement of three thousand years, in another crumbling rubbish. So it is in the spiritual world: in the ultimate forces which make mankind and produce a State. Proportion determines: number rules.

In Europe as a whole religion is to-day marshalled in two camps, mainly regional. The one is that which has kept in continuity with tradition, and comprises France, Belgium, Spain, Italy, the Valleys of the Rhine and the Danube, and Ireland. Throughout that region there is a minority, always very small (insignificant in Italy and Belgium and Spain, less than three per cent. in France, much more intermixed upon the Rhine and the Danube), which takes its character from the Reformation, and is, in ethics, if no longer in doctrine, Protestant; but the tone of all that region is traditional and Catholic: nor is this truth affected by that by-product of Catholicism which we call anti-clericalism. A man of this culture may most sincerely hate the organisation and power of the Catholic Church; he may combat it to the full as a tyrannical and degrading falsehood (such is the mood of what is called "Anti-clericalism"), yet will he show in all his manner of speech and in all the fundamental social ideas which he takes for granted, that he is of the traditional culture and alien to

the Protestant north.   Monsieur Clemenceau is
an excellent example of what I mean by this.
Further, the small Protestant bodies within the
Catholic culture of Europe, even where they
have great power through their wealth, as in
France, are strongly affected by the social
atmosphere around them.   In general you may
say (under all those qualifications which are
necessary to any simple statement of a complicated organic thing) that Europe south and
west of a certain line is Catholic.

Similarly you may say that Europe north and
west of a certain line is Protestant.

That line is accurately traced on the very excellent German modern atlases, where difference of religion and every other point on which
statistical information is available are set forth.
It is a line running first west of old Serbia, then
following the Danube, and (roughly speaking)
the Carpathians, cutting across Galicia, and going nearly straight northward to within a day's
journey of the Baltic; thence it runs westward
through the mountains which frame the Bo-
hemian plain, then turns north again towards the
mouths of the Rhine, passes down the English
Channel and rises northward again to include
Ireland, with the exception of the planted north-
east corner of that island.

The Protestant religion gives you England

and Scotland, the Northern Netherlands (that is, Holland), North Germany, Scandinavia, Finland and land south of the Gulf of Finland.

The characteristics of this culture as a whole are its high proportion of industrialism. In its agricultural part, under suitable conditions (such as Norway and most of the Protestant Swiss district), a highly democratic organisation of peasant owners; but under the more complicated conditions, which are the rule, an aristocratic organisation: the land held by a wealthy governing class and the mass of the people working under them as dependents. Further, during the last century, the centre of gravity of Europe in wealth, and in other social factors more and more until the Great War, lay within the Protestant north. The Catholic south, even with the inclusion of France, became more and more imitative of the Protestant north. The latter affirmed its own superiority and believed in it, while the former was subject to violent internal strain through the great quarrel everywhere at work (but first of all in France) between the organisation of the Catholic Church and the Civil Power. Moreover, the two typical instances of Ireland and Poland up to the Great War affected the mind of Europe. Both were subject Catholic nations, controlled against their wills by powers alien to and inimical to the Catholic Church. Many of the Poles, of course, had the privilege of a milder subjection within the Austrian Empire, where they exercised considerable power. But the intensely Catholic western section of Poland was under the heel of Berlin, and the no less intensely Catholic Irish were under the foreign government of London. No corresponding subjection of a Protestant society to one of Catholic culture existed, and such a picture affected the general judgment, tending to persuade it that the one culture, the Catholic, was declining, the other, the Protestant, advancing.

Now in the United States there was no such regional division. That Continent (it is no less) presented a totally different arrangement of spiritual forces. The main of the country's tradition was Protestant, and even Puritan. The spiritual forces opposed to this tradition—active scepticism upon the part of an important few, the Catholic organisation of many millions —were scattered, interpenetrating the whole body; regional indeed to this extent, that the Catholic forces, weak or almost unknown in vast agricultural districts, were always powerful and sometimes overwhelming in the great towns. But there was (and is) in the United States no distinction by district between a Catholic and a Protestant culture. The culture of the whole was Protestant; the Catholic element, comparatively recent as a weighty factor, was a dispersed minority controlling far less than its numerical share of wealth and influence.

Here, then, was a balance in proportion; a setting together of elements quite different in pattern from what ruled in Europe: a system which you may find in certain small districts of Europe, but not in Europe as a whole. The Protestant capitals of Europe are conscious of the Catholic capitals; the two spiritual forces in Europe are polarised, and reactions between the two camps are continual and active. There are no Catholic Capitals in the United States.

When we turn to the special contrast between the United States and England, we have another set of arrangements to consider. England has been from the Reformation until quite recent times an essentially aristocratic State. It is still aristocratic in all its traditions and structure; and it is even possible that in spite of the growth of the great towns, and the present decline of the aristocratic spirit, its degradation into mere plutocracy and the forgetfulness of old relations between the governing and governed, the aristocratic spirit will return. It is not perhaps probable, but it is possible; and at any rate the old aristocratic framework of England is still everywhere apparent.

This historical process is expressed in England by the institution of the Church of England. Establishment and endowment are not the chief marks of this institution, which has not its like in the world. Its chief mark is the way in which this organisation is coincident with what was, until recently, and still largely is, the governing part of the nation.

No doctrines define the Church of England. Its ministers may and do define doctrine as each wills—save, of course, the anti-national doctrine of papal supremacy. What all agree in is the *National* function of the establishment.

Official ceremony, great national functions, the villages and country towns from which all England sprang, and which are still the preservers of the English soul, have the Church of England for a medium. More important still, the great "Public Schools," as they are called, wherein the wealthier class is trained in a fashion so sharply different from the education of the mass of the people in the Elementary Schools, these are almost universally within the organisation of the Church of England. The independent, or free Protestant bodies, what are commonly called in England the "Nonconformist bodies," arose in protest against the existence of a State Church—not nearly so much in protest against doctrine as in protest against an alliance between the Civil State and the Church. These great communities were at their origin in conflict with the State Church, and later, when the conflict had ceased, were still in a lesser social position; the nation was not officially expressed through their action.

With all this there went a highly concentrated unity of national type, produced by what was, in spite of domestic differences which loomed very large at home, an essentially united national religion. The English character and ethics were and are everywhere unmistakable, and are the fruit of a common religious experience.

Now of this arrangement the United States not only bears no trace, but has even no comprehension. Very few indeed are those American citizens who have lived so long in England, or have become in any other fashion so familiar with the English spirit, that they can even recognise the point I am making. Such a thing as a governing class, as the training of that class in special schools, as its connection with the State through a religious organisation, not of doctrine but of practice and habit, is not only unknown to the average American but fairly inconceivable to him. It means a different world. The Free Churches are not, in the American mind, connected in any way with the idea of protest against the State or against any

form of social or political power or superiority.
Springing from various equally free sources,
the various Protestant bodies in America have
united, or, rather, are already in fusion. On our
side of the Atlantic they have sprung from different levels, and were, and still are in great part,
stratified.

Lastly, there is this profound historical difference in the religious development of the two societies. In England a great mass of the populace
—to-day the majority of the populace—was and
is unaffected by the Established Church on the
one hand and the Nonconformist bodies on the
other. It has long been indifferent. Whereas
in America the great mass of the populace,
nearly all that part of the people who are settled
on the land, and, until recent times, the town
populace as well, were steeped in an active, accepted, and taught form of set doctrinal religion.
This contrast does not appear upon the surface,
because the depths of society take long to affect
the surface, but it is there. The average American of pure American descent, though his people
should have been poor for generations, is of the
Puritan religion. Your average English work-
ing-man is not. The Puritan religion with us is
middle class. In America it was, and still largely
is, popular; and anyone who will meditate upon
that contradiction will see what effect it must

have in these coming years when everything shall abide question.

One very striking effect of this contrast between the United States and England, an effect which must necessarily bear great fruit in the near future, is the corresponding contrast between the sceptical movement in America and in Britain.

Roughly speaking, outside the Catholic Church to-day throughout the Occidental world, throughout Christendom, scepticism is universal. *Faith* has everywhere yielded to *Opinion*.

The definition of Faith is the acceptance of a truth, and the refusal to entertain the possibility of an opposite to that truth, although proof is absent. Faith must be coincident with reason, but it is not established by reason. Science is the acceptance of a truth, and the refusal to admit the possibility of an opposite, because conclusive proof has been presented, and reason has accepted that proof. Opinion is the partial acceptation of an affirmation, the opposite of which is still regarded as possible.

The modern world, I say—the modern Christian world—(using the word Christian in the cultural and not in the doctrinal sense) has lapsed from Faith into Opinion, outside the Catholic body.

So true is this, that the very quality or defini-

tion of Faith which I have just given appears
to-day, outside the Catholic body, absurd; and
though all men are making Acts of Faith all day
long (as, for instance, the universal Act of Faith
in the existence both of themselves and of the
world outside themselves—neither of which can
be proved) yet they have lost the knowledge that
those acts are acts of faith at all. Science and
Opinion alone are conceived to cover the whole
field. Faith is unexperienced.

Now in this situation England will, and must,
behave as the rest of Europe behaves—that is,
the loss of faith produces rapidly in England as
in the rest of Europe a revolution in ethics; and
the Pagan origins from which we sprang, noble
and ignoble, reappear as the poor remaining
fragments of Christian dogma are abandoned.

But in the United States it is not so. The
modern sceptical movement, the substitution of
Opinion for Faith, leave the ethics of the nation,
not unchanged indeed, but still in an unbroken
tradition, and that tradition is essentially Puritan.

The second point I made at the outset of this
difficult piece of analysis was, that the United
States present a religious contrast to Europe,
and especially to England, in the fact that their
religious experience is isolated; that the reaction
of Catholic culture upon Protestant is hardly

felt; that certain consequences of religious difference which we in Europe had known for generations and allowed for were, in the United States, hitherto unknown, have but recently appeared, are still novel and as yet not fully analysed. Of these by far the most important— so much the most important that it covers all that is worth noting in the field— is *the necessary conflict between the Civil State and Catholic Church where the two are not identified.*

The Catholic Church is in its root principle at issue with the Civic definition both of freedom and of authority. For the purpose of the State, religion is either a universally admitted system, or a matter of individual choice. But by the definition which is the very soul of Catholicism, religion must be for the Catholic *First,* a supreme authority superior to any claims of the State; *Secondly,* a corporate thing, and not an individual thing; *Thirdly,* a thing dependent upon Authority, and not upon a personal mood; *Fourthly,* a guarantee of individual freedom in all that is not of Faith.

Harnack uttered a profound truth in what he intended to be a sneer, when he said that men either had their own religion or somebody else's religion. The religion of the Catholic is not a mood induced by isolated personal introspection coupled with an isolated personal attempt to dis-

cover all things and the Maker of all things. It
is essentially *an acceptation of the religion of
others;* which others are the Apostolic College,
the Conciliar decisions, and all that proceeds
from the authoritative voice of the Church. For
the Catholic, it is not he himself, it is the Church
which can alone discover, decide and affirm.
Moreover, the Catholic regards that which is so
decided and affirmed as good and salutary, forming the only home of the human race, outside
which are but puerilities or despairs, and he regards that which denies or combats such Authority and such affirmation as evil in its consequences and destructive to the dignity and right
ordering of man. Lastly, the Catholic instinctively feels his right of personal choice in all that
is not defined by creed: *e.g.* in the matter of food
and drink.

Now it is clear that between this attitude and
the attitude of a non-Catholic State which pro-
poses "tolerance" (that is, the definition of all
religion as an individual concern), there is conflict. For "tolerance" means indifference to
those acts and doctrines which the State treats
as private, *coupled with enforcement of certain
acts and doctrines which the State insists upon
treating as universal.*

I am not here concerned with the evident
falsehood of this word tolerance. I use it be-

cause it is the current word for this particular attitude which every State, not identified with Catholicism, must take up.

I repeat, tolerance means to-day, in the mind of the modern statesman, and particularly in the mind of the American citizen, the enforcement of certain doctrines and practices, and, side by side with these, a complete freedom in such doctrines and practices as lie outside those limits.

For instance, the American State enforces the doctrine of private property; the doctrine and practice of monogamy—not of monogamy in the sense of tolerating only one living wife, but in the sense of not tolerating two legal marriages with one person at the same time. It also forbids the purchase and transport of wine, but not those of Mrs. Stopes' books, etc.

Up to the present day the position of the Catholic in the United States has insecurely fitted in with this modern conception of tolerance, through the fact that the dogmas taken for granted by the State, and enforced in practice, were mainly Catholic dogmas; and that the action of the State, where its dogmas differed from Catholic dogma, was mainly negative and permissive.

But such a state of affairs cannot be permanent; and to prove that it cannot be permanent I will give two examples.

It may well come about, at any moment, that the State shall pass a law compelling those who have the guardianship of human beings incapable beyond a certain degree to see to the removal of those human beings. The State may take it for granted as a universal doctrine, to be held and enforced upon all citizens, that the preservation of imbecile or imperfect life, much more its continuance from one generation to another by the propagation of children, is destructive of society; and it may order that these unfortunate beings be placed in what is called, in our modern scientific jargon, the lethal chamber.

Now for a Catholic to act in this fashion is, by Catholic definition, *murder;* and what is more, any action supporting, or even permitting this thing, is also from the Catholic point of view murder. If A. is a Catholic receiving an order to put out of life the imbecile B., he not only commits murder if he obeys, but he commits murder if he hands over the imbecile B. to the State official C., whom he knows will so act. More, he will be committing murder if he does not do everything in his power to *prevent* the official C. from carrying out the law.

I have chosen this extreme and violent example because it is particularly illuminating; nor can anyone say that it is fantastic, seeing

what things are proposed to-day and what ideas
are becoming familiar.

But I can give much nearer instances. A
law forbidding a minister of religion to marry
two people unless they were certificated by medi-
cal or other authority would not, and could not,
be obeyed in the Catholic community; nor could a
law in any way artificially restricting the birth
of children.

If an actual example be demanded, we have
one before our eyes in a proposal which has already arisen in the matter of education in the
United States. It has already been proposed,
and may at any time become law, in certain
parts of the United States, that a parent should
be forbidden to send his child to any but one
particular type of school agreeable to the State,
and shall be compelled to send his child to that
school. The State here affirms the doctrine and
practice that a certain religious atmosphere is,
or should be, universal to the human race; or,
at any rate, to all its citizens; which religious
atmosphere is other than the Catholic. Such a
law no Catholic would obey; for, by Catholic
definition, it is the parent who should decide upon
the education of the child, not the State.

In general, that conflict with which Europe
is acquainted to the full, and which has filled

the history of two thousand years, from the time of Nero to our own, is inevitable.

Now we in Europe, being so familiar with this, taking it for granted, and knowing that the conflict is always potentially present, arrange for it in various ways; by certain compromises and anomalies in one time; by vigorous persecution in other times; by accepting corporate union between the faith and the civil power. In all these ways the strain is resolved or postponed, and an equilibrium, stable or unstable, preserved. But no one can know the United States without admitting that when the conflict shall there arise, an equilibrium will not be established or preserved, for the conflict will be novel and will seem monstrous. On the one side you have a plain affirmation that the law is the law and must be obeyed, and indignant surprise on the rejection of what seems so obvious and universal a rule. On the other, you will have, as you have had throughout history, resistance to and denial of that rule.

The chief political problem presented by religion has, then, still to be solved in the New World. What the result will be certainly no foreigner could attempt to predict, and probably no American citizen who has recognised that problem from his reading of history, or from his instinctive reaction against the presence of the

Catholic Church, can foretell one either. But presented the problem certainly will be, and in one or other of the many fashions, stable or unstable, more or less tragic, it will have to be solved.

I must close with this suggestion, putting it so that it shall be as inoffensive as possible, though I fear there must always be some note of offence in it. The new and separate spirit which has made America, which creates a spiritual condition peculiar to that Continent, may produce, perhaps will soon produce, at any rate *tends* to produce, some quite unique experiment in the field of religion.

We have had islands, as it were, of such experiment in more than one case; but seeing the way in which great waves spread suddenly over that field of a six score millions, seeing the rapid intensity and unity of their action, I cannot but think that the future holds some rapid, and to us of Europe startlingly new, American growth: a new body and organisation in the domain of religion. Not an isolated, fractional experiment, but a great national or cultural invention. A new Religion. Should such a transformation come, then the conflict with Catholicism of which I have spoken must arise immediately and in its severest form.

VII

THE CONTRAST IN THE JEWISH PROBLEM

I SAID in a previous chapter that the candour of American society—one of its chief marks —was apparent in their treatment of that great problem which the whole world is now discussing, and which rises in importance with every passing day, the problem of the friction between the Jewish race and those among whom they live.

It is but one point out of many, but it is a point of such special prominence in the United States to-day that it merits a brief section of its own.

As might be expected, in a community where every public thing is freely discussed, where government is not in the hands of a secret clique, and where all men expect, as a right, the power of administering the common weal, the Jewish problem has come, in America, right up to the surface of public discussion and attention.

Here in Europe, though it is no longer driven underground, it is dealt with by the public journals very timidly. While it takes a larger and yet larger place in conversation, the expression of it in our printed word, which is our modern medium of communication, lags far behind.

The old "Liberal" humbug of the mid-nineteenth century still affects us largely in this matter. It does not affect the Americans at all. The commercial reason for silence—the newspapers' fear of losing advertisement revenue—affects them as it does us—but less than it does us. The personal reason, fear of the Jewish power and respect for convention, affects Americans hardly at all in this regard. They are accustomed to saying what they think, and there never has been with them as with us a social convention or taboo forbidding all debate on the subject. The result is a situation the like of which we have not in Europe. To put it plainly, the Jewish problem is discussed in America openly and publicly, with as much eagerness and as much downright emotion as it is discussed in England secretly and privately; it is a universal subject to which all men's minds are eagerly turned, and the effects of this new interest—for it is of recent growth—cannot but be considerable.

I take it that during the first hundred years and more of independent American national

life the Jewish problem was in no way acute.
With the Americans, as with the high civilisation
of Western Europe, the French, the English,
the Spanish, the Italians, the Jews presented
themselves only as a small, and, upon the whole,
wealthy body: with them as with us, the hypocrisy or illusion which pretended that the Jewish
definition was religious instead of racial lasted
long. With them, as with us, a strong and gen-
erous doctrine in favour of any minority which
suffered from the dislike of the majority, had
great weight and produced a patience that was
akin to virtue. I am afraid this was not always
a virtue practised in favour of minorities really
unpopular; for instance, the Mormons in America
or the Irish in Great Britain—still, a vague
ideal of sufferance (not defined, and therefore
capricious in practice) not only protected but
actually supported the little Jewish body in the
New World.

In the last twenty-five years, and acutely in
the last five years, all that has changed. One of
those mysterious migrations which the Jewish
race undertakes from time to time—such a
swarming as that which led them in hordes to
the sanctuary of mediæval Poland, or such a migration as had earlier brought myriads of them
into the valley of the Rhine—led this unfor-

tunate, uprooted people to seek refuge in the
United States.

At once, as is always the case when a great
body of Jews appears suddenly in any community, the Jewish problem arose in all its intensity.
The Jews are now about one-third of the city of
New York.   They threaten, or are said to
threaten, to occupy a predominant place in certain of the American Universities.   They have
great power over the Press, a still greater power
over finance; they have their measure of power
over the professional politicians—not indeed the
complete power which they have over here, but
an increasing power.

Against all this the American, who is the most
nationalist of modern men (and that is saying a
great deal!) violently reacts; and the consequence
is that the Jewish problem is discussed all over
the north-eastern States with violence, and elsewhere with a permanent and acute attention.
The Jewish problem is at least as important to-
day in New York as was in Paris during the
nineteenth century the question of the suffrage,
or as was in Manchester and London of the
same period the question of Protection and Free
Trade.

I will bargain that there is nothing which
seems more surprising to the average Englishman upon his arrival to-day in the United States,

when he engages in conversation with some average American whom he meets without introduction in the course of his travels, than this
universal preoccupation with the new problem
of the Jewish immigrants.

Now before we can understand this somewhat
surprising and, I fear, disturbing state of affairs
we must understand what parallel there is to it in
Europe: and here again, as in the case of the
military experience discussed elsewhere, there is
a distant parallel with the French, but none with
any other European State.

Let us put the matter first negatively. In the
United States there is *not* any such attitude
towards the Jewish problem as you have in
Europe east of the Elbe. Though the new influx
of Jews is enormous in New York, and dis-
quieting in certain other eastern cities, it has not
numerically affected the bulk of the population.
They are not, as in Roumania, in Poland, in
Lithuania, in the Ukraine, and even in some parts
of the German States, so numerous as to affect
the tone of the population and to make the whole
Gentile community organise in its own defence.
You have that in New York alone, and even in
New York defensive organisation is only just beginning. Apart from the fact that the number of
Jews in America is small compared with the total
population, there is the American habit of flux,

of human beings perpetually passing from place
to place, which makes even the congestion of
Jews in one eastern town less formidable than it
would be otherwise. Men say: "For the moment
there is heavy pressure; but the new element will
spread" (they never say it will be absorbed), and
they also say: "We have seen many other floods
of immigration, and they have always been spread
at last over the mass of our community." The
Jews are, if I am not mistaken, to-day less than
three per cent. of the community, much less than
what they are in Poland and only a little more
than what they are in the German States; and it is
rather from congestion in a few places than from
mere numbers that there has arisen the acute
irritation to which everyone visiting America
bears witness.

Next let it be clearly understood that the
American Jewish problem is *not* in any way
parallel to the same problem in England. It is
absolutely essential to understand this, for nearly
all our public men make such mistakes over it as
to ruin their policy. Not a few of them will come
to America and make their first stay in some
Jewish banker's house, a choice which damns the
chance of their future appeal to American opinion. In one notorious case an English professional politician enjoyed a sort of triumphal
march through the New York ghetto, from the

landing-stage to the Town Hall, and our newspapers religiously noted it as an expression of
American opinion. The inter-mixture of the
Jew with the wealthy governing families, which
has gone so far in England that it is the note of
all English society to-day, is quite unknown in
the United States. In the Oxford and Cam-
bridge colleges, the great clubs, the crack reg-
iments, the Public Schools, in all the bodies
associated with wealth in England, the Jew has
now an established and honoured place. A certain
proportion of Jews has become a necessity to
those corporations and to the governing class of
England as a whole. But the Jew has no such
place in the United States. He enters the great
American clubs with difficulty, from most of
them he is barred; his talent is little used in the
staff work of the army; he has not a true civic
position at all. In our great families inter-
marriage with Jews has become so common, or
even so necessary, that, as I have said, nearly all
of them now show Jewish blood. The American
great families (if I may use such a term of a people so egalitarian—I mean the old families of
the South, the two-hundred-year-old families,
Dutch and English, of the eastern seaboard)
have not a trace of Jew about them, and would be
indignant at the suggestion that any of them
showed the least sign of Jewish blood.

Lastly, there has never been in America a political alliance comparable to the long-standing political alliance between the English State in its external or foreign relation and the Jewish financial interest. The Americans have known nothing of such typical combined action as the Rothschild loan and the occupation of Egypt.

On the other hand, Americans have never had an active conflict between the Jewish race and its hosts such as marks the history of nearly every group in Europe. The Spaniards, after centuries of half alliance, turned to persecution; the English, after a violent exile of every Jew from their shores, turned to an alliance; the Poles, after making themselves a City of Refuge for all the persecuted Jews of Christendom, became the victims of their own generosity, and are to-day suffering for it most manifestly. But in America there is no historic tradition of this kind; there has been no conflict hitherto with the Jew; the friction is novel. It is the more intense, and at the same time the more naïve and crude. Therein also lies a peril, for the American does not know, as we of old Europe know, that you cannot deal with this terrible problem in a rough-and-ready fashion. He does not know, as we know, that it always begins by seeming insignificant, then disturbing, and at last feverish. It is a novelty to him which has come quite suddenly, and which he takes in full front as is his habit.

And here we come to the positive side. There are I know not how many hotels in America which refuse to receive Jews. As I have already said, the principal clubs refuse to receive them; the Universities, notably Harvard, have openly organised a defence against the invasion of further Jewish students. Most significant of all, in spite of what advertisement means to the modern Press, and in spite of what abstract finance means to concrete production in the modern world, we have had the significant episode of Mr. Henry Ford.

That most competent manufacturer, and certainly honest man, found, late in life, and in the midst of his career, that there was such a thing as a Jewish problem. The Jews attacked his business upon the general principle of cheapening an article, and then buying it up when it had been so cheapened. He put up a fine fight and won; but he was not content with winning upon his own ground, as most men would have been; he carried the war into Africa. In this, I think, all men must respect him, for he showed tenacity, courage, and clear thought. Mr. Henry Ford seems to have said to himself: (1) "This people will return; it is not enough to repel an attack, one must follow up one's victory." (2) "I have discovered a public danger which I am determined to expose." Mr. Henry Ford thereupon, in the *Dearborn Independent,* took up the cudgels against Jewish power. It was a minority battle, and remains a minority battle. It was unlike anything we have in Europe. The defence against Jewish aggression upon the Continent of Europe is an intellectual and moral defence. No very rich man as yet has dared to take part in it. In America, in the hands of Mr. Ford, it became a financial defence. A very rich man indeed came out to battle on the side of his own people.

Now Mr. Ford's action was only one part of the whole movement. On account of its directness and intensity, the Jewish community in the United States has chosen to exaggerate its proportionate value. It is a strong defensive weapon to direct the public eye upon one's most active opponent, perhaps one's most exaggerated opponent, and thereby make men forget every other aspect of the battle. The attempt was made to represent Mr. Ford as an isolated, ill-balanced man with no supporters. That attempt has failed not only in the United States, but also in the eyes of all visitors to the United States. It is quite clear to-day that the average American is moved by the increasing friction between his people and the Jewish nation.

Now that being so, what is the force which has hitherto prevented trouble? It is here that the French parallel comes in. The force which has hitherto prevented trouble (I do not say that it will permanently prevent trouble from breaking out, for the Americans have a way of acting, and soon come to an end of words) is the sacredness of a certain specific doctrine: the presence in America of something like a civil religion. In France the Jew has been protected by a political creed widely spread among Frenchmen, a collection of dogmas derived from the great Encyclopædists of the eighteenth century, and established in arms by the soldiers of the Revolution. These dogmas affirmed universal citizenship, and affirmed that there was no exception to citizenship. A man once admitted a citizen might express what opinion he would, and, so long as he obeyed the public law, was entitled to protection. He might be of any race under Heaven, black, yellow or white, but so long as he was admitted a French citizen he was entitled to as full a protection and to as many rights as any other.

Precisely the same civic dogma influences the American mind; it is one of those innumerable points in which the great Stoics of the eighteenth century proved themselves the spiritual fathers of the French as of the American Republican breed. Under such a doctrine there is no room for action against the Jew, or the Negro, or the Chinaman, or any other alien. He may be refused entry, but once he has been admitted to the city, all the rest follows.

Whereas in France this doctrine prevails against all others, in America popular feeling does often take the reins, and that is why some have thought that the friction between the Jewish race and their hosts will break out into violence in America before it breaks out in any other part of the world. That is why some have thought that the increasing strain would come to a head in the United States before it came to a head elsewhere.

I, for my own part, am not so sure. I do not pretend to speak for a society which I love, which has done me every kind of good, and the sincerity of which fills me with admiration, but which is foreign to me. But judging the matter as a foreigner, I should say that there would be no action in America against the Jew. There may be laws against him, using the word "against" in the sense of laws of segregation. There may be occasional anti-Jewish outbursts, but I do not expect (it is a purely personal judgment) such a movement against the Jews as took place against the Mormons, or such universal modern uprisings as have taken place against the threats of disruption to society. I think matters will go, upon the whole, peaceably. They will *not* go upon the old nonsensical lines of pretending that a Jew is not a Jew, and that his presence in the commonwealth is indifferent to that commonwealth; that neither I nor any other man can believe. The problem will probably be solved, as it should be, in peace, and by special laws. A great effort is already being made to prevent further undue immigration; it is already fairly successful, and as yet no injustice or unreasoned action has been permitted.

I may sum the thing up by saying that I, as a foreigner, think so well of the United States, that I believe the solution will there be found, as we ought ourselves to find it in Europe, by the honest admission of the Jewish problem, by a respect, and even for those of us who feel it, an affection, for the Jewish people; by a determination to allow no mood of folly to upset the settlement; and by that settlement taking the form of a recognition of a separate community resident amongst its hosts upon clearly defined terms. We are a long way from that yet, but it is possible and we must hope that it will come. For the alternative is a tragedy.

*   *   *   *   *

I have written this chapter subject to the knowledge that though all men *speak* of it, anything *printed* upon this matter, at this particular moment, will be travestied, ridiculed, caricatured, and that open public expression and judgment upon one of the gravest of modern political difficulties will be freely lied about or treated as a jest.   I cannot waste time upon such follies. Everyone now-a-days has the Jewish problem in his mind or on his lips; it is very serious and important; and no one can write of the United States in especial without giving that problem its right value.   If I be asked what I most desire, I have expressed it; if I be asked what I have seen and heard, I also express it.   I confidently leave it to the future to prove if I am right as to what I desire, and to fulfil what I hope, which is that Israel may have peace.

VIII

THE CONTRAST IN LETTERS

1. *As a Cause.*

THE study of a people's attitude towards
Letters when that people has settled into
a final form is of the first value. The same study
applied to a people still in process of formation
is perhaps less conclusive, but it is of some service.

In the first place the literature of a people tells
us a great deal of their character, and in its subtleties can even reveal the ultimate springs of
that character. It tells us something of the road
by which they have travelled to their resting-
place. It is also—if we are dealing with a people of the past—the main (sometimes the sole)
evidence we have of their character. Of a people
arrived at maturity and no longer surviving in
the modern world we may say that we hardly
know them unless we know their literature, and
that if they have a full literature, and we know
it well, then we know them fully. Of a contemporary people this is also true. Though it is not

so essential with them as with a people of the past
to judge them through their literature, yet it is
their literature which is their voice for us. That
is why our foreign politics are always badly conducted if they are conducted by men who do not
know the literature of the contemporary foreign
nations with which they are dealing. But with
a people in formation it is otherwise. Their
literature is nearly always in some degree derivative: that is, given to them as a somewhat alien
thing, or at any rate a distant thing, and proceeding from others who are not themselves.
Even when it is not derivative it is imperfect.
Further, a people in the making has much more
of its energies devoted to the very business of
making itself than it has to the business of expressing itself.

On all these accounts it is wise not to exaggerate the function of literature in any study
of the American people to-day. To depend
upon that evidence mainly would be a very bad
guide indeed, for in their case more than in the
case of any other nation we know in history there
are present all those characteristics which lower
the value of the literary test. They still have
much dependence upon "loan" literature; they
have been engaged, and are still engaged, upon
a vast physical task, and a vast political task corresponding to it, which is more important to

them than expression; they have not a pretence
to, they would not themselves claim as yet (for
it would be absurd) an indigenous, isolated, separate, literary fruit. That will come, but it has
not come yet. Lastly, the process of differentiation has, as yet, proceeded so slightly, that the
judging of the Northern English-speaking
Americans by their attitude towards Letters,
and the making of this judgment apart from a
knowledge of their real life and manner, is more
warping than a similar judgment would be, applied to any other modern or ancient people. If
the American nation had produced by this time
a literature quite distinctly different from that
of Europe, it would but be a beginning. So far
not even this stage has been reached.

The very fact that foreigners so perpetually
judge the American State by its Letters would
almost persuade me to avoid any examination
of this field; so grotesque have been the judgments passed and so insufficient in any case is
this field for a proper examination of the main
Contrast.

Nevertheless, the Contrast in Letters between
the New World and Europe is, I think, of sufficient value to merit a separate examination.
It does not tell us much, but it tells us something; and especially may those who speak the
same language in the Old World learn some

humility and acquire at least a hesitation in their pronouncements, by considering in its detail the literary situation of the American people.

The attitude of any community towards letters is, to those studying that community, useful in two fashions. They may consider Letters as a cause moulding and creating the people which use them. They may consider Letters as an effect: as a proof or symptom: as a method of discovering what the soul of the nation may be.

The prose and verse which people read mould them in some degree and direct their activity; in this they are a cause; but it is also true that a national spirit chooses what it will read, and letters are an effect of that spirit.

I will take the lesser first, and consider the function of literature as a cause affecting the character of the American individual and of the American State; we shall discover there also that Contrast the portrayal of which is the object of this book.

I note, in the function of Letters as applied to the American individual and State, five capital points which I will first tabulate and then discuss in their order:—

1. The Classics—the antique masterpieces of the Mediterranean—are not with America, as they are with us, the root in continuity with which all Letters stand.

2. The more or less conscious, the more or
less present, reaction of contemporary languages
and literature upon one's own—which reaction
is a necessary mark of every community in
Europe, and by which, indeed, we in Europe
mainly judge the value and profundity of any
individual's culture—is not present amongst the
Americans; or at any rate in nothing like the
same degree. *Their* reactions are from within;
they take place as between various sections of
the American people, various strata of American
society. They do not come directly from the
French, the German, the Italian, the Spaniard,
the Slav; and even the indirect effect of the non-
English contemporary world is distant and slight.

3. The conditions under which American
society grew, the vast distances traversed and
colonised, the foundation of innumerable lesser
and greater centres of population (in a country
where it was shameful to be illiterate) lent
especial vigour to the *ephemeral* forms of literature; by which I mean not the forms of literature
destined soon to die on account of their weakness
and insufficiency, but the forms materially
ephemeral—the newspaper, the magazine, the
topical book.

4. In contradistinction (but not in contradiction) to the last point, you have the fact that
these innumerable centres, spread over a very

large area, led to the actual personal purchase
and possession of books, as distinguished from
the European institution of the Library; and this
has had a very great effect indeed upon the character of American reading. Not that the American lacks libraries. His towns have larger and
better endowed libraries by far than ours. But
he purchases also and possesses books in every
station of life, where we should borrow.

5. There has been for the Americans so far
(it may not long continue) what I will call, for
lack of a better metaphor, a *refraction* of literature.

Like all new things worth expressing, this
thing is exceedingly difficult to express, and I
have no great talent for discovering new methods
for the expression of new things. I will develop
the point more fully later on, but for the purpose
of this table I may say that I mean this: The
American Commonwealth, determined to avoid
illiteracy, necessarily deriving from one European State alone most of its original literary
"stock," tended to distort it by simplification of
the many and subtle English shades of meaning
and connotation. It tended also to distort, in
what was becoming a more and more alien society, the relative places of English writers, to
make rigid imaginary literary values and to
create, as it were, a Canon. It tended to estab-

lish as certain and fixed and much upon one level a body of English literature (not all of it excellent, by the way, but most of it excellent), and to imagine a gulf between this and all the rest. The American mind, at the origins of its modern culture, tended, from its connection with English literature, coupled with its distance from the original source, to put into two separate compartments books supposedly beyond criticism and books supposedly of a very different and lesser value. One might put it in another way by saying that America tended to make of certain English examples what the English and all other European nations make of the Latin and Greek masters; at the same time, the relative values of English work were often lost.

Now if we go over these five points we shall discover, I think, the action directed upon the American mind by its use of letters, especially during the nineteenth century.

1. There are very many scholars in the United States whose acquaintance with the Greek and Latin classics is as great, and whose power of criticism, literary and textual, is as high as any in Europe. The contrast does not lie here between the proportion of those who are acquainted with the origins of European Letters, but rather in the continuity with these origins. We in Europe all instinctively refer to Latin

and Greek.   The man most externally proud of
his ignorance of Latin and Greek is, in his heart
of hearts, ashamed of that ignorance.   There is
with us an unceasing effect of the pagan classics
permeating down from those who are expert in
the dead languages to the mass of the community.   We feel in Europe that to cut ourselves off
from such a spring is to run the risk of becoming
a desert.   We are in touch with a not very remote past when Latin was a universal language,
and our scholars are perpetually passing on the
Greek influence to us also.   It would take much
more space than this book allows to give a sufficient body of example, but over and over again
you find in European Letters, no matter how remote they be from the true source, the echo, the
recapture, the inheritance, the filial recognition
of our divine ancestry in Athens and in Rome.

There are all sorts of little social ways in which
the test may be applied.   For instance: the man
who has been loudest in proclaiming that the advance of physical science has rendered classical
learning insignificant would probably be ab-
surdly ashamed of himself if he were caught
making a false quantity in a Latin name.[1]   Or,
again, each of our European governments, after
it has passed beyond a certain degree of folly in

---

[1] I can picture Mr. H. G. Wells' expression if he were
caught saying Pápy̆rus for Papy̆rus!

diminishing the classics in the programme of official education, halts and goes back to the better tradition.

Now that backward-looking spirit is absent in the modern American. The great mass of modern American thought (and here I fear I shall offend many) even at its highest is indifferent to the ancient roots upon which we in Europe depend. It has begun afresh (if indeed that be possible) not with a language sprung from its own soil, but with a language already developed and put into final form by the English at the end of the sixteenth and the beginning of the seventeenth century.

2. I have said that there is a corresponding difference between the American and the European effect of foreign literatures. In Europe our occidental culture (and to this we must add in some degree the Slavs) reacts perpetually, unit upon unit. It is true that the languages are now so finally formed—the High German, the King's English, the Academic French, the Tuscan Italian, Castilian—that they no longer largely intermix, largely lend words one to the other or largely change the one the other. The future historian will, indeed, find this, I think, a curious and rather baffling phenomenon peculiar to our own times, that these five or six great standard languages should co-exist in a

common civilisation and percolate so little each
out of its water-tight compartment into the rest.
But the thought, the expression, within each, is
of immediate and violent effect upon the rest.
You may take two such cultures, so different
(and antagonistic in many ways) as the French
and the English, and yet find at any moment this
reaction in full swing. Kipling is translated into
French by a man of genius, so that his work is
much better reading in French than in English.
That towering masterpiece, Bédier's *Tristan et
Iseult,* provokes at once several English trans-
lations of high rank. Such a man as Claudel
recognises, and is steeped in, Keats. Such a man
as Swinburne goes a little mad over Victor Hugo.
D'Annunzio was the rage at Oxford when I was
a young man. The German idioms peculiar to
what passed for philosophy in Northern Germany
are still commonplaces of Balliol talk; and even
the puerile sterility of Herbert Spencer was
familiar to the Continent of Europe. One might
extend the list indefinitely. All the European
literary units, at least six in number (and one
might add a seventh, the Scandinavian) react
perpetually one against the other within a closed
field. Nor does English (as many imagine)
escape this general fate. Indeed, English letters
receive the foreign spiritual (not literal) impres-

sion more perhaps than French—certainly more than Spanish.

But in the case of the United States this reaction fails. For a certain small number it may exist, but their influence does not percolate to the mass. The European reactions affect the United States somewhat in the long run but only through the channel of the English tongue, and, in the main, after passing through English sources.

There are exceptions, I know. I will myself quote what has always seemed to me the most striking, that very fine piece of Catholic Slav work, *Quo Vadis?* Being Catholic, it was sharply boycotted in England. It was forced on us here in England by America. It was an American translator who discovered the book, and it was through American enthusiasm that it was reluctantly admitted into England. But such exceptions do not contradict the general truth: that the direct reaction from the various continental literatures upon American literary expression is slight. That which comes comes mainly through the channel of English.

On the other hand, there are, as I have said, very strong reactions from within, and every American keen upon the literature of his country will point out to you the influence of this society, of that climate, of the other economic conditions,

the influence of the New England tradition, of
the Virginian, of the Pioneers of the Pacific
slope and of the Middle West—and so on: so
many forces from within, moulding, changing,
developing the Letters of his country.

It is significant, indeed, of the contrast between
America and Europe that to us in Europe these
terms which are of high vital import to the
American judgment are without meaning. The
well-educated Englishman will tell you readily
what it meant that Maeterlinck should recently
have admitted, and subscribed to the influence
of, Charles Maurras. He will trace the effect
of Ibsen upon some German or of Tolstoi on some
Dutch contemporary. But should you ask
him whether such and such a work published in
modern America showed the influence of this
or that school or this or that local tradition, he
could tell you nothing about it. The types are
quite unfamiliar to him. Their history, their
social relations one with another he knows
nothing about—and cares less. These American
nuances are a world apart from the modern
Englishman, and, of course, from the German,
French, Italian, Spaniard and Slav. I say again,
the reactions of American letters are from within.
That these internal influences are powerful and
creative I know by the testimony of those who
can understand them, but I can also bear witness

(which will be endorsed by every honest European not pretending to know more than he does) that they are a sealed book to us of Europe, and the more American literature develops the less we understand the regional influences at work in it.

It would seem in connection with this second point which I am making (that reactions in America are from within, but in Europe are at work between half a dozen national units), it would seem, I say, from this that the Americans would in time produce a completely differentiated literature of their own. That indeed I believe, as I shall have occasion to say a little later on, will be the case; and if that development *does* take place it will be largely due to the absence of those external—what we call in England "foreign"—forces: the German, the French, the Spanish, the Italian, the Scandinavian, the Slavonic thought; at least from the absence of those forces coming *directly* upon the Letters of America.

One European group alone has direct influence, and that is the English. The oddest political results flow from this truth—as, for instance, the conception held by many Americans that England is a democratic country. But with these I am not here concerned. I am concerned only with the fact that of all European groups one only can directly affect American letters; and that is the English group. I notice that the effect even of this gets less and less with every passing year.

3. The third point which I made, the necessary emphasis upon the ephemeral *format,* due to the rapid spread of population over great areas and the formation of so many distant new centres (coupled with the determination to prevent illiteracy) seems to me to have two hidden but powerful sources.

The first source was a more or less conscious determination to maintain national and social unity in spite of so wide a dispersion. This spread everywhere the use of a topical source of information and instruction. The topical newspaper, the topical magazine ran through pioneer America, spreading westward, and inevitably became a social habit. It was one of the bonds which kept together that amazingly rapid expansion. And the second, even less conscious, force at work was what I will call the force of flux. This American life, in which a man was born in one place, uses his activities in half a dozen others in succession, and died perhaps on the edge of an unexplored world, made for rapid succession in the thing read, parallel to the rapid succession of experiences in the life lived. It made for "news." It made for the reiterated experience

of the weekly and the monthly bundle of reading
matter, perpetually extended.   I think—though
it is very difficult to grope down to the roots of
these things—I think that these two forces, in
varying degrees of consciousness, were mostly at
work in producing the dominance of the ephemeral *format,* the magazine and the newspaper, in
American society.

The prevalence of these in Europe (where
they have nothing like the same extension) came
to us as a habit learned from America.   It is not
native to us.   The forces sustaining it with us
as a novel habit are the unrest of our great towns.
Our peasantry, our settled population, is not
much taken by the ephemeral *format*.   It largely
does without a daily paper.   It is not even much
attached to its weekly paper.   But in the United
States the ephemeral *format* in literature is universal.   You find the passion for it just as
strong in the settled population of long standing
upon the land as you find it in the towns.

Now the effect of this as an agent is considerable.   It means that the mentality of the
reader is affected as by a constant stream playing upon him.   It explains the very great power
of advertising over such a population, and it goes
with the power of suggestion in other channels.

It is in some degree (but this has been much
exaggerated) antagonistic to those forms of

literary work which may be called lapidary;
which require great recollection and detachment.
On the other hand, it exercises something of the
functions of a sieve. Matter thus present in
ephemeral form must, so to speak, pass through
a certain mesh. It cannot be, it may not be, as
its detractors pretend, below a certain level; not
indeed of literary or moral excellence (it may be
as base as possible), but of interest and appeal.
It is significant in this connection that the best
illustration being done on a large scale in any
country in the world is done in America. The
quality of illustration in the monthly magazines
and the daily press is on the very highest level.
I have by me a sketch of a dozen people waiting
for a train: a sketch drawn, half in jest, for one
of the popular New York papers, one of those
papers in which our own politicians write, and
which make the least pretention to culture; yet
Forain himself would not have been ashamed to
sign this sketch.

4. I have said that a further mark of American Letters as an agent is the personal purchase
and possession of the book, that is, of the permanent literary form. This is not in contradiction of my last point. The powerful forces
which have established the ephemeral form of the
newspaper and the magazine throughout the
American Commonwealth, with all the good and

evil attached to them, have not prevented this spread of the book. We writers of Europe note with avarice and astonishment what the circulation of a book in the United States can be. We see that when a book has "caught on" the Americans will buy a hundred copies where in England we buy a dozen, and those who know America well readily testify to the truth that this personal purchase and possession of books arises from the combination of a constantly reading population with great distances and a great number of centres of population.

I have always thought it amusing that the library habit, through which we European authors starve, should be associated with the name of an American millionaire. The library in our small, densely-packed countries, notably in England, multiplies circulation without multiplying the author's (or the publisher's) profit. It gives you twenty or a hundred readers for one volume, where, but for it, you would have, say, ten volumes purchased. But in America the library, as I said above, does not do this. Though the whole Commonwealth is studded with public libraries, large and small, though the possession of a public library is a sort of decency which no place dares deny itself, under peril of losing its reputation, yet the American will personally buy and possess the book he desires to read.

But there goes with this a singular vice: inherent to the great distances, the unrest and the flux—the three determining conditions which have also made the American newspaper and the American magazine—and this vice is the vice of uncritical exaltation. A book among the Americans "takes" exactly as fire "takes" in dry gorse. It is not true that merely bad stuff takes because it is bad—people who pass this judgment are talking demonstrable nonsense. But it is true that a book of no permanent value, possessed of some vivid stimulus which will not exercise itself beyond a very brief time and which tends to no particularly good end, will pass through an untold number of hands in a few weeks. One sees, in America, the popular book of the day standing in great stacks upon the counters, not so much of book stores as of drapers (or dry goods) and every other kind of salesman.

I have noticed for myself (but I put it tentatively, since I am writing of a country so very foreign to Englishmen)—let me say that I *seem* to have noticed for myself—that this vice does much less harm than might be imagined. Our popular atheist literature on prehistory and geology sells hugely; but I doubt whether it has much affected American religion or even the most superficial American thought. On those who already believed what some "best seller" was repeating to them out of bad text books it could have no effect, for he was already upon their level and they upon his; but I noticed when I discussed the effect of one such book with those who formed part of the vast purchasing army, that they had not been converted by any argument, nor had swallowed whole any new statement they had found therein—or rather, to be exact (since there were no new statements and no new arguments in it, but merely the re-hash of the materialist guesswork of our time), let me say that I did not find a single man of Christian tradition moved by this book, although myriads of such men had bought it.

Now here, as it seems to me, America is singularly fortunate compared with ourselves. If in England a book is widely bought, whether it be a work of fiction based upon a certain philosophy, or a book inculcating directly a certain philosophy, that philosophy is spread by the book. In America, as it would seem—why, I know not—the effect is far less. One might disrespectfully compare the American attitude in this point, I think, to another national habit, that of chewing gum; or to the habit common to the whole human race, that of eating sweets. In America these books of wide circulation are read, but not very much remembered—and that is all to the good. On the other hand, there is a large and permanent purchase of good classical English stuff, under this drawback, that it works too much by label. Certain names of certain books become established without the direction towards them or their successors of a critical faculty—and that is all to the bad. It is natural; it is inevitable.

The distance between America and England is one of many thousand miles in mere space; the spiritual distance is greater still. Men cannot put upon their shelves as stock classics Racine, or Tasso, or Cervantes, for these foreign languages have no avenue of approach to them. They put therefore Shakespeare and Milton and Tennyson. But they tend to take their Tennyson whole—and that is an error. It is mistaking a false for a true category. They tend, do the Americans, more than the mass of our purchasers here in Europe (and we tend enough to it, Heaven knows!) to judge the wine by the label, instead of by the taste—at least where foreign and especially English work is concerned. With the work of their own countrymen it is necessarily otherwise. *There,* judgment is more personal and accurate.

5. The fifth point which I made is (as I said when I first put it down at the head of this chapter) very difficult indeed to define. I have called it the "refraction"—or distortion—of English

literature in the United States: the turning of
a number of varying values into one or two sets
of values, and these *not* the values of the orig-
inals in their own habitat: the simplification or
annulment of all those nuances and all those
shades of expression which the native Englishman discovers in proportion to his critical faculty: the transposition of *our* values, making
Tennyson's "Brook" a greater poem than the first
chorus in "Atalanta," or the death of Little Nell
superior to Sir John Moore's in Napier.

I say again the thing is inevitable. You are
dealing with literature at second hand, and literature at second hand must always go through this
process. But it is a pity. I have sometimes
thought it would be better for both parties, the
American and the Englishman, if the vast political difference between the two could be reflected
in the literary field. It sounds like a blasphemy,
but I am not sure that it would not be better for
both parties if the very Englishry of, say, Dr.
Johnson, made the American avoid his Boswell,
for, as it is, the American who is receiving things
through a foreign medium receives them somewhat distorted.

I will give two examples which I hope will
be sufficient. A novel of Mrs. Humphry Ward
will be taken seriously among the Americans—
yes, among the most cultivated Americans; yes,

among the Americans most possessed of irony and of touch. But how many Americans could savour such a masterpiece as *The Diary of a Nobody?* Very few, I think; for the simple reason that *The Diary of a Nobody* derives its whole literary excellence from a profound penetration of that highly local, national thing, English suburban, middle-class life; a thing as remote from American experience as anything one could conceive.

And there is another example. The Americans, with some of the finest examples of political oratory present before their eyes, printed from the lips of men born upon their own soil, will none the less accept as an orator any tawdry parliamentarian from our side. They accept a label only; and they accept it because it comes from a foreign source, but from a foreign source speaking a language which is their own.

This particular (and, I think I may say, distressing) note in American letters will not last. The moment a native literature arises, sufficiently differentiated to challenge the imported thing, the insufficient value of the import will be seen—or rather there will come a tendency to neglect even what is good in the import. Certainly there will be no remaining tendency to pretend or accept admiration of what is insignificant. But, while it lasts, this phenomenon whereby literary matter received from a distant and alien source is accepted by, though transformed in, a foreign mind, disturbs and warps the literary temperament of the United States; and it is a pity.

II. *As an Effect or Test.*

I have said that the attitude of a community towards Letters regarded as an agent in the forming of the national life, a cause, is of less importance to a foreigner attempting to understand that community than are letters regarded as an effect, a test of the nation's soul and character. It is certainly so in the case of the Americans.

When we desire to appreciate the strong and rapidly growing differentiation of the New World we do well to ask what action upon that phenomenon Literature may have had, but we get much more light when we consider the literature read and written by Americans as an instrument of analysis; as a measure by which we may gauge what is happening in the development of the American mind.

Now in this direction there are three main points which everyone, I think, discovers at once when he watches the American mind at work upon modern Letters. Each of these three bears witness to the ending of one epoch and the approach of another; the ending of an epoch in which Letters had not that distinctively national quality which all the other Institutions of the State already possessed, and the beginning of another epoch in which such a distinctive character will most undoubtedly be present.

The three points are these:—

1. The outstanding typical names which may be quoted as the chief in American prose and verse are of a past definitely closed; and a complaint arises here, in England (where so little is known or understood of the New World) that the American literary faculty has declined and is dying. The complaint is ill-founded and ignorant; but it is symptomatic of change that the leading names belong to the past and that there has been now a considerable period in which no second group of such names has arisen; there is a gap such as comes nearly always before a revolution in letters.

2. The second point is the increasing conventionality with which the American monuments of the past are received to-day by the American mind. The names go on; but they are not the seeds of future work; they are becoming more and more names only. That is highly significant, it is the very mark of a change. It is *more* a mark of change than if those names or labels

had come to be despised—that they should be, so to speak, sterilised, or, to change the metaphor, that they should have become fossils, revered fossils, is immensely to the point.

3. Modern America is full of an incipient but eager and even violent creative ferment in letters, which is so entirely its own that (*a*) the foreigner cannot judge it; (*b*) it hardly crosses the Atlantic.

Now all these three phenomena, and they are undoubtedly the prime phenomena at the moment in American Letters, point to the same thing. The differentiation of the New World, its launching out into a sea of its own, the approaching recognition of its complete severance from our own, is clearly manifest in all these three things. I make bold to say that the very ignorance and fatuity of the criticisms passed in Europe upon modern American work are yet another indication of this truth.

Now let us consider these three points in succession:—

The first has been a commonplace for some time past. Pretty well any English critic will tell you that American Letters have died out. Not only are all the leaders dead, but the English critic finds none to replace them at all. Here and there an individual English best-seller, mindful of his American sales and fearful of losing a market, tries to flatter the Transatlantic writer of English by assuring him that this or that particular American writer is a newly-revealed genius. The greater part of English critics do not indulge in this unnecessary flattery, and those who do are not only unnecessary but wrong. It is not true—judged by any permanent literary standard—that modern America has yet produced any great leading names or work which is likely to prove permanent.

Here I am on very thin ice, for the American world is already so utterly removed in spirit from our own, that to apply our standards to it even in the most general form is perilous; still, the judgment seems to me sound, that, so far, the gap continues and is not bridged. There is a group of considerable writers all dead, and there is no apparent carrying on of their tradition, just as there is the record of an American social life now quite dead and in its place the great cities of the present. But I take it that this gap or halt is not to be compared to such fatigues or diversions of the national mind on its literary side as marked England, for instance, in one generation of the eighteenth century, or as marked the art of the Dutch after their great triumphs of the seventeenth century, or as marked Spanish prose after the great triumphs of the same period.

As a test of the truth of this I put the following question: "Does anyone believe that after the lull or gap, or whatever you call it, through which American Letters appear to be passing the tradition will be recovered, a continuity re-established with the men of the middle nineteenth century, a reaction towards the older and more English manner developed?" No one can believe this, everyone must admit either that the gap, or lull, has come to stay and that American Letters will produce nothing more (a conclusion which seems to me at least fantastic, and even absurd, given the intense energy of the nation and its manifest creative power), or he must admit that something new will follow the present hesitation. It seems to me as certain that something new will come as that the new great cities have already come.

We have here one of those many cases in the analysis of society where general prophecy is well assured but particular prophecy impossible. No one can pretend to say by what avenue, let alone in what shape, the new creations will arrive. They may come through a political avenue under the stimulus of political change; they may come in connection with new religious movements; they may come (and this is the more probable, for it is the way in which leaders have arisen elsewhere) through the influence of one genius or of a group of such, quite apart from

the stimuli of changed political or religious conditions. But through whatever avenue the new
creations arrive, or in whatever unknown form
they manifest themselves, this much is certain,
that they will come with vigour and that they
will be totally, startlingly *new*. It may be that
they will be so new that Europe will reject them
with contempt—a fact that would not affect
them much. It may be, on the contrary, their
novelty will strike people with amazement, and
even with admiration—a much less likely event.
But, at any rate, it is hardly conceivable that
they should not come. Everything is ready for
them, the whole air of the place is one of expect-
ancy. The fuel is there: nothing is needed but
a brand.

2. The fact that the older models essentially
English in character have turned to fossils, that
the titles are alone revered and the content within untasted or found distasteful, is again a proof
of this contention: the contention of existing contrast soon to express itself violently in matter
and form.

I said just now that this phenomenon was the
most characteristic of all; it is not comparable to
the common phenomenon present in all societies
whereby the literature of the immediate past having grown familiar becomes dull and at last neg-
lected until reaction takes place and there is a

return to it. It is not comparable to the phenomenon, for instance, whereby the earlier Victorians in England lost their comprehension of Pope and Dryden, or that whereby the Georgians (as they call themselves) have to-day lost their comprehension of Tennyson. If the modern American mind, on its literary side, were reviling the old English models, whether those arising on their own soil or those inherited from ours, that would be a sign of the normal contempt which each generation feels for the immediate past. But what is happening is far more significant; the old models are still revered by *name*. It would seem as though the younger Americans make an effort to recapture as a matter of duty the emotions which they once aroused, and though they make that effort, fail.

I did myself, alas! in the course of a little address provoke very great irritation by saying something which I still believe to be true, and which goes to the very core of what I am now trying to express. What I said was this, that if a reciter gives Keats' "Ode to a Nightingale" with the accent and manner of American intonation, rhythm and all the rest of it, which makes the spoken American tongue so different a thing from the spoken English tongue, that great poem becomes cryptic in English ears. I cannot but believe that recited in the English intona-

tion it must sound foreign in American ears.
The great Gettysburg speech afforded a sort of
breach or transition. It was of American origin,
though its form was still of the English classical
type; but if you recite a *modern* piece of level
English prose in the American manner and in
American surroundings it loses its quality altogether; and if you recite some one of the later
American passages in prose or verse which has
moved the modern American mind it will sound
to an English ear not only unfamiliar but uncon-
vincing and spoken, as it were, to an audience
with whom the hearer had nothing in common.

I say this judgment provoked my hearers to
lamentable irritation; but why? Because among
those to whom it was addressed (many years ago)
there was still a very strong tradition, which has
by no means died out in the United States, that it
was a duty to "react" to Keats with the "reactions" of an Englishman. To say that the power
of doing so was passing away sounded like a blasphemy; yet I believe that it was true.

To this judgment I will attach another of
which I am fairly sure, and this is, that the
French or Italian scholar fully acquainted with
the English tongue derives from reading the
"Ode to a Nightingale" an emotion almost exactly correspondent to the emotions of an Englishman. We are all European together, and

that Greek antiquity which at second hand in-
spired Keats inspires in a similar fashion all the
culture of Western Christendom. But in America it is not so. You might to-morrow (I had
almost written *will* to-morrow) have another and
another and yet another Englishman or Frenchman or Irishman recovering, exalting, and illustrating that same tradition. A French writer
may be writing to-morrow not only on the level
of, but in the full tradition of André de Chénier
or Leconte de L'Isle; an English Parnassian
may arise to-morrow with the same restrained
forms and the same inhibiting passion as Dryden,
but America will not give us resurrections of
this kind. When America begins to give us Letters which are the full expression of a mature
national personality we shall have something that
does not derive from any such sources, but from
the genius or influence of its place of birth.

The last character confirms that conclusion;
it is the character of converging, corporate activity which you find at a buzz throughout the
younger writers in America to-day. It seems to
me not indeed certain but probable, so probable
as to be *almost* a certainty, that this intense
activity, this clash of minds, this sharp succession of experiments will lead on without a break
to some synthesis of all that power, to the action

of some one or few pens in which that new mind and that new shape shall express themselves.

I here may refer to those two matters which I have already noted in this connection, the fact that we of Europe, and especially of England, fail to follow the new literary activity of America, criticise it wrongly, misunderstand it or (what I hope are the wiser among us) forbear to criticise it because we do not understand it. Side by side with this is the corresponding fact that the new American work does not cross the Atlantic.

When I last visited the United States, a few months ago, the question I was most frequently asked was what I, or at any rate English writers of my time, thought of the modern American writers. To this I could only answer, quite truthfully, that we did not think anything. We did not understand the movement; and if I, personally, or indeed any one of my contemporaries were to attempt to pass judgment upon the new thing he would be dealing with matters so alien to him that his judgment would be worthless. I for my part could make no pretence to saying whether this writer or that among those of the younger generation of the United States were the leader or had the greater chance of permanence. I could not even say honestly which I preferred; I could only say that there was here a new thing acting by new standards and, what

is much more important, springing from a root
unknown to me: informed by a spirit which had
never been within my experience. It is not a
paradox to say that this very incapacity to judge
is a proof of capacity to affirm the contrast.
Were a man of a generation ago hearing the
music of Wagner to say, "To me it sounds like
nothing but noise, I do not pretend to understand
it," that would be proof that a new thing had appeared. It would not be a paradox to affirm that
his incapacity was in itself a proof of his judgment when he said: "I affirm that a change has
come and that something new has appeared," and
to this we add the admitted fact that this new work
does not cross the Atlantic; we still export (I do
not know how long it will continue) our English
stuff, even the little that is good in our English
stuff, into the United States; but the United
States does not export to us anything save what
amuses us for a moment in some mechanical form
of humour.

I will bargain that a collection of those idio-
matic intensely national stories sprung from various regions of the Republic, which all visitors to
America remember to have followed with imperfect appreciation, I will bargain that a collection of these brought over here would fall quite
dead; and with every passing decade the difficulty of presenting an essentially national Ameri-

can piece of work to an English audience increases. So true is this that the literature (if it can be called literature), the journalism rather, common to the two societies has been reduced to the very lowest possible denomination; nothing but the crudest sensationalism expressed with the most violent emphasis can be said to discover a *common* audience upon either side of the sea. The worthy work fails in that regard. Here it may be asked, why if we Europeans are incapable (as we most undoubtedly are!) of seizing the American spirit in Letters, America should itself import, as it still does, so much indifferent and even a little good English work? I imagine it to be in part the effect of tradition, in part of routine, in part of that natural looking towards an older society upon the part of a younger; but I confess that it always astonishes me.

For instance, I understand that they have sold in great numbers in the United States a book dealing mainly with the English gentry in an English Cathedral town, and I know that there sells still in great numbers a set of books dealing with one particular section of our agricultural people. It is evident that the readers of these books can have no communion or sympathy with the subject. They are more remote from the English Cathedral town and the particular bit of West of England agricultural country in question than would be a Russian; and if a demand for work of this kind still continues, as it does, beyond the Atlantic, I do not see upon what the demand can depend save tradition, routine and the natural interest in, or respect for, something old which lies behind one's own civilisation; nor can I believe that the demand for this sort of thing will long continue. But can anyone conceive an American parallel with a corresponding sale upon this side? Yet I should say that, upon the whole, the analysis and presentation of social detail in America were more vividly given in American literature than those of England in our own. It is certain that the demand over here for a corresponding American work (much smaller though it be than the American demand for our work) results in hopeless misconception. No one gets a greater shock on visiting the United States than the man who has read upon this side before visiting them descriptions of this kind: descriptions by Americans of American life.

One might sum up the whole of this discussion by saying that if the United States were using as a medium of expression a language of their own to-day, there would be already apparent the novelty and the isolation of their literary faculty: that the New Thing would already have appeared. One might add that, because the medium of expression is linked with one of the

European languages and is even mechanically identical with it, the appearance of that New Thing is delayed.

But come it must. Like every other witness to reality the shock of its coming will do more good than harm. It will help us to undertake the task which for most of us is so hard and even repugnant, *the task of learning once for all that the American people possess another, and a foreign, culture.*

IX

A NOTE ON LANGUAGE

MEN say nowadays (though they never said
it when it would have been a useful thing
to say) that we of Europe would be more modest
in our appreciation of the New World, less hostile to it, more interested in The Contrast, if
we discovered a foreign language as the vehicle
of so completely foreign a society. That is true.
The similarity of language warps all our alien
judgment.

And here let me consider in great fear and
trembling this problem of language. In great
fear and trembling because it is a matter where
men's affections are deeply involved. I will only
write what has affected myself in the matter,
very humbly, protesting that so individual and
partial an impression is to be received but as a
grain of testimony. Thousands of men have each
had their varied impressions of the thing: but
for what my impression may be worth, here it is.

*   *   *   *   *

Let me begin at the beginning, with the obvious. That will preserve me from two very bad

forms of error: First, a paradoxical contempt
for what one knows very well to be true and
what one's readers also know to be true, but
which we writers tend to neglect just because it
is so well known: Next from that error which is
even worse, I mean reliance upon the obvious
alone; for if we state at the very beginning of
any exposition what our starting-point is, we
shall recognise it for a starting-point and not mistake it for the goal.

The obvious thing which we all know is
that the British and the Irish speak a
tongue which is "the same" as the tongue
spoken in the United States. Admit the well-
known little exceptions, the fragment of original
dialects, called "Celtic," in the West of Ireland
and Scotland, and admitting the interest of the
Welch language on our side and of small islands
of French and one or two other European idioms
in America, it remains true that when the plain
man says "all these people, British and American,
talk one language, English," he is telling the
truth.

It is even true that the mere phrase "English
speaking world" is a just description of Britain,
great parts of the British Empire, Ireland and
the United States, although the use of that
phrase as a *political* category leads to the most
absurd and dangerous errors.

That is our starting point: the language is the same. But on this foundation we have to erect a series of observations upon the contrast present here also between the two sides of the Atlantic.

To appreciate that contrast let us eliminate for the moment a certain factor which I will consider later, but which, as regards the *spoken language* (that is the *living* thing) is an obstruction or a false guide—I mean the printed word. What does an Englishman first notice on landing in America as the contrast between the two sides of the Atlantic so far as the *spoken* language is concerned? The first thing which strikes him is the violent contrast in intonation; the next will be the considerable contrast in vowel sounds; and the next—which will not strike everybody at first, but which will strike anyone who pays careful attention to the detail—is the modification already apparent of certain consonants in the popular speech.

Now it is to be remarked that, so far as we can now judge, the probability is that various languages in the past have grown out of a common stock through growing differences in these three things and in that order of importance: first, the changed intonation; next, as a result, the changed vowel sound; lastly, certain (much slighter and less numerous) consonantal changes separated the Greek and Italic dialects, and made French, Castilian, Tuscan, out of Latin.

Before people write a language down, one set of them, being removed from the rest and mixed with other blood under another air, will begin by putting a different *intonation* upon the words they use. This leads mentally and at once to a differentiation in vowel sounds. And when they come, much later, after the change has widely developed, each to write down his own speech, the differences have already produced appreciably different languages.

On writing down the new words on each side, long after the differentiation has taken place and has developed, you get apparently different formations. For the vowels change very largely. They are the most easily affected of the sounds which make up human speech: The modern English "Courtesy," the old "Courtoisie," "Beef," "Bœuf," "Siege" (of a town), "Siège" (*d'une ville*), etc.

Lastly, even the consonants change. And these change in a very odd manner, which would seem capricious. Men have tried to make laws about it, but they are none of them convincing. One set of people takes, we know not why, to omitting some consonant they find too hard to pronounce, or liquifying it or aspirating it; and the process goes on with many consonant sounds until a com-

pletely new word appears when it comes to be
written down.

If you want a strong and first-rate example
in the concrete of what this means, take the English word "Bishop" and the French word *Evêque*
for the head of a Christian Diocese. The French
word may be simplest set down in the English
tongue and English letters thus "ehvehk." That
does not give you, of course, the particular vowel
sound of the French, which is very different from
the English "eh," and in the French word the
second "eh" is broader and more open than the
first. But it is a fairly accurate transliteration
of the French name for this exalted being. Now
the English word for the same may be accurately
set down "Bish'p," that is the way in which a
fully cultivated English man pronounces the
word spelled "Bishop." Now, look at those two
words, "ehvehk" and "bish'p." No two could
be more different! If you came across those two
words in two primitive dialects, where record
had perished and where no earlier writing was
there to guide you, you would be quite certain
that they came from two quite different roots.
Yet both come directly and by gradual change
(in not more than fifty generations) from exactly the same original. That original was the
Greek "episkopos." The French word originated
in a certain trailing of the syllables in intonation,

while the Saxon intonation became apparently
more and more brisk. The last syllables of the
word got slurred in the one intonation as in the
other. But they were apparently lost after the
"k" sound in the middle in one case and not till
after the labial "p" sound in the other. Meanwhile the "p" at the beginning of the word was
hissed into a "v" in one case and flattened into
"b" in the other. In the French case the "k"
sound was so strong that the "s" before it was
gradually dropped—it was in fact only dropped
quite recently—in the last four hundred years.
In the English the "k" sound was kept for a
long time, but so was the "p" sound at the end,
"Biskop." You had in the French case "epis-
copos" gradually turned into "esvesk' " with an
apostrophe or dead sound after the "k," the "s"
at last dropped and "ehvehk" as the final form.
In the other, English, case you had all the consonants kept accurately, but the vowel sound at
the beginning and at the end dropped. Then
you got the trimmed form "Biskop" at last
slurred into "bishop," and finally the strongly
accented first syllable cut very short, and the
"o" sound turned into a short almost elided "u"
sound till you get "bish'p." And there at last
are your two forms of the original Greek word
as different as chalk from cheese, yet both de-

rived (as innumerable records prove) from the same original.

*   *   *   *   *

When an Englishman lands in America he has difficulty in understanding the sentences spoken around him. The populace, speaking a familiar phrase quickly, seem to him to be speaking a foreign tongue, and he himself must often repeat what he has to say to be understood. There is already as much differentiation as that. And the differentiation has come, as always, first from a very marked change in intonation, next from a considerable change in vowel sounds, and lastly from a slight but already perceptible change in consonant sounds.

There are, of course, many ways of pronouncing the same printed words in different parts of the United States and in different social bodies within the same part of the United States. The race of the immigrant affects his speech, and so does his calling and his degree of culture. Allowing for all that, these three differences have already taken root.

How great the change in intonation is, only he can appreciate who will carefully analyse the rhythm and the tonal quality of some phrase identical to the two branches, English and American. And there is not only a difference in rhythm and in tonal inflection, that is in the musical

notes of a sentence, but there is also a spiritual
difference in the motive. Different parts of the
same phrase are emphasised. That means not
only a difference in the sense of rhythm but some
subtle difference in the mind of the speaker. So
far as rhythm is concerned the main difference
would seem to be that one which I have said may
be discovered in many other departments of the
national life beyond this medium of speech. The
American rhythm is shorter. If you hear an
Englishman pronounce a long sentence, such as,
"I shall be very glad to see him again after such
a long interval," and then compare it with the
way in which upon the average an American
would pronounce identically the same printed
words, you will discover, I think, that the number of emphatic syllables in the English intonation is less than in the American.

To take a metaphor from the movement of
water, the waves are shorter and steeper. Further, the phrase lifts in tone at the end in English and falls in American. And on top of all
this there is a very marked difference of what is
called "accent," which is mainly the difference
in vowel sound.

Now the differences in vowel sound are innumerable, and I cannot pretend to classify
them. It has been done by those who have given
special attention to the science of language; but

I do not, and I think that every careful observant from our side will note how every vowel sound without exception has taken on this side of the Atlantic some different value from what it has upon ours. And in many cases the change is so great that the exact setting down of it in an accurate transliteration would involve a totally different spelling.

There is the difference which is beginning; as yet barely perceptible. If I should quote instances I should be told by any American reader that I was taking them from loose, ill-educated talk, which was not characteristic of the true language. But such popular change must inevitably become a general change. Even in carefully-pronounced words, traditional and in the mouth of a highly-educated man, a slight consonantal change is apparent. Notably the characteristic "th" is generally less aspirated. (I mean, at the risk of giving offence, that it becomes nearly a pure hard dental like "d.") "The" has not yet become "de," but it is on the way.

Here, however, in the matter of the consonant, comes in that other factor of the printed word. The fact that the common language has also a common script has established a million regular checks arresting change. Print does not prevent vowel change, because vowel change comes unperceived. It is subject to an indefinite amount of modification without any necessity for re-spelling. An educated Englishman has come to say "clark" where the mass of his fellows say "clurk," but the spelling remains the same. If he found himself drifting into saying "clar*g*" the spelling would correct him, but in the case of the vowel it does not. To pronounce "the" like "de," however strong the tendency may become, would remain a shameful thing for the educated man, who would always try, even when the differentiation had become strong and dominant, to recapture the old characteristic sound which was there before him in print as a guide. On the contrary, these very short "clipped" vowels of the cultured English are already beginning to sound ridiculous in American equally cultured ears: especially our very short "o." Conversely, our very long "a" has begun to have a ridiculous sound in the same ears. It sounds there almost like "aw": a braying.

So far, therefore, as differentiation of language by mere pronunciation is concerned, we seem to have a process of this kind developing, but not rapidly developing, along its own lines: (1) A grave and increasing difference in intonation; (2) already considerable difference of vowel sound; (3) a *very slight,* perpetually checked, differentiation in some few consonantal sounds.

However far the process goes, the common

printed word will maintain a continuous bond wherever the same vocabulary is used. I therefore conceive that, short of a very possible accident, which I will discuss in a moment, the differentiation will hardly proceed, even after a long space of time, say ten more generations, to a point where the one spoken language shall become unintelligible to the other.

But vocabulary is not in the same case; and the causes of a change in vocabulary are deeper than mere new habits or new objects to be named. The English and American vocabularies are drifting apart, not so much because there is a different set of things to be named as because there is a different set of moods to be expressed.

I think I here notice one curious symptom, which is the greater American reliance upon the substantive as compared with our reliance on the adjective. I further note this factor: that words admittedly slang and base fall into the language capriciously in spite of protest.

Here is something to which no man can give a law. The causes at work are too many, too ephemeral, and too sudden in their action to be connected in one system. It has been so with all changing languages. Thus in the dialects which sprang out of popular Latin a few obviously slang phrases become words of capital importance. The word for eating, for instance, in the popular Italian and French dialects clearly came from what was originally slang, but now quite replaces the older classical word.

You cannot say what part of the popular illegitimate new growth which is perpetually rising and dying on either side of the ocean will remain. But you can say (1) that a certain small portion will remain on each side, (2) that the portion which will remain will be *different* in either case, and that will cause, even if things remain as they are, a considerable divergence.

It has already caused a divergence so great in one particular department that every Englishman landing in the States notices it at once. That is in the department of the newspaper phrase designed to convey an immediate impression. I will take you at random fifty headlines and as many separate sentences from a dozen papers in New York or Chicago, print them as they are, and set them as an examination test before any Englishman who has not known America by travel or by special reading, and that man will fail to pass in the examination.

What would he make of "Pastor scores ball fans," or "Pearl case Sleuth's frame-up Countess says"?

Lastly, there is a category of words to which I pay curious attention because they seem to be such strong symptoms of the difference between the American speech and our own; and that is the group of differing words attaching to objects *equally common* to either civilisation. There are here two categories; the names of new things and the names of old things.

If there is one thing, for instance, which you would think an American and an Englishman would call by the same name it would be the fuel of the internal combustion engine. Yet to the one it is *gas* and to the other it is *petrol.*

If there was one object of our generation which you would have thought identical in name as it is in character to both sides of the sea it is a street vehicle, running on rails and having electricity for its motive power. But to one it is a *trolley* and to the other it is a *tram.*

Each civilisation has recently developed, or borrowed, what was originally a Parisian system of housing, living not under a separate roof with one's own front door, but on one floor of many in a house. But to one his little horizontal home is a *flat,* to the other an *apartment.* When an Englishman hears that an American friend is living in an "apartment" house it sounds mere tautology. For apartment with us means a room, and he takes it for granted that houses have rooms. He has to learn that it means what he calls a flat.

A "lift" is an "elevator," and (what is really

astonishing!) a Catholic priest is frequently a "Pastor!" That is sound enough in theology, but a very great shock when you first hear it. For, to the travelled Catholic Englishman, there rises up with that word a hideous vision of the Huguenots. It is as though an American Baptist visiting England were to hear one of his Ministers called Monsignor.

In this matter of language modern man will ask a writer of any book, even of this poor book, a certain question. Those who have struggled through my pages so far will be framing that question and asking me to answer it. The question is, *"What of the future?"* In vain do I answer on this as on most prophecies, "We don't know." I fear that I must attempt some satisfaction. I will suggest, then, not a definite reply but a statement of possibilities and probabilities.

So long as you have the two factors of (1) an inter-communicated and printed word, (2) a high and connected civilisation, it would seem probable that what may still be called a common language will survive. It may rapidly become of difficult appreciation in speech—when I say rapidly, I mean rapidly as spaces of historical time are counted. It is already something of a task for the general population of the one place to understand the general population of the other. But the common printed word and the inter-communication of a high culture would present so strong a similarity as would prevent full separation. *If* communication, full communication, survives, America and England will long have the same tongue, although the Englishman on first coming to the United States does not even to-day understand most of what he first hears on the lips of the populace.

But it is not the experience of mankind that a high culture and continual inter-communication can indefinitely be maintained. It is the experience of mankind, on the contrary, that these things go in great ups and downs, that men get interested in other things, in new religions or in new conflicts. It is the experience of mankind that a period of high and intense civilisation wears out and is followed by periods of repose, which we should call to-day periods of decline.

The distance in mere miles is very great, the form of communication most precarious: apparently easy under the conditions of to-day, but sinking at once to peril and chance adventure if or when our great machines lose their quality. And should the level of our material culture, the intensity of our present inter-communication, seriously lower, *then* it would seem probable, and highly probable, that the languages would rapidly differentiate.

A short century of even partial isolation

would produce two tongues, with a common script, but with vocabularies largely dissimilar, the spoken word wholly so. A short century of isolation would make the one group incomprehensible to the other.

X

THE FOREIGN RELATION

THE relation between the United States and the European civilisation from which its culture originally derived has no parallel in history. Not only is it impossible here to judge from past examples of colonisation and expansion, but attempted judgment based upon such apparent parallels misleads us altogether.

The characteristic differences between the position of North America in this regard and anything in the past are these:—

1. The emigrant or descendant body has very quickly achieved a complete separation from its source. It is a separation absolute in kind and not (as have been all past parallels) in degree.

2. It has increased numerically and generically, both absolutely and relatively to its original stock, out of all proportion to any other parallel relation between descendant and original. I say "numerically and generically." If we look at that increase as a whole, not merely in area, not merely in numbers, but in novel ideas

and transformed ideas, in wealth and in the direction of energy, there is no parallel to it.

3. (And this I take to be of great importance)—The increase began coincidentally with the achievement of real separation: that is, something novel was at work which was the common cause of this strange, unexampled, rapidity of increase, and this strange unexampled rapidity of differentiation.

4. (a) The physical constitution of the Commonwealth, its human stock, the forms of the Commonwealth, its political traditions, its ideas derived from Europe as a whole—from the occidental culture, from Christendom; yet (b) in proportions other than those of the parent continent; while (c) the *origin* was *mainly* derived from *one* province of this Europe alone, to wit, Protestant Britain: one highly diversified society out of all Europe.

The English relation of the United States is, therefore, unique. It gives to the general foreign relations of the American people a set of forces quite different from those affecting the foreign relations of any people in history. They begin with blood largely English, with institutions largely English, and language all but identically English. But this small original was leavened, while it so vastly grew, with ideas all foreign to the English people and many of them repugnant to that people. The actual physical ingredients, the proportions of the stock, have changed. There has not been the mere expansion of one set of colonists upon its own lines, the simple multiplication of a primal blood. There has been an immense admixture of other stocks, nearly all of them other than, most of them highly antagonistic to, the original stock.

Now you will probably find one or another of these four elements present in certain historical parallels; you might even find, I suppose, with a sufficient knowledge of antiquity, a parallel to the complete isolation or separation of the descendant from the original. But a combination of the four points you will find nowhere in history nor anything like it; and that combination is intimate and decisive. It makes of the American Commonwealth a unique thing.

From the fact that the United States are European in origin you have all that group of major phenomena which make the United States part of what we loosely call "the white civilisation." It has also been called by a piece of historical guess work "Caucasian" or "Aryan" —words that mean very little. If we want a word that is roughly accurate historically and roughly corresponding to reality we must call it either "Occidental Culture," as I have done (for it is sharply defined in history as the culture of the Atlantic and Mediterranean confines of the great land group in the northern old world), or better still (though the implications of the title will shock some people), the Græco-Roman culture.

But if we are exceedingly courageous, and make so bold as to talk plumb history without fake of fine words and humbug, why then we must call it *Christendom*.

At any rate, we all know what it is, and the United States are part of it; but they are part of it subject to a cultural schism, the intensity of which it is my whole object in these pages to emphasise and declare. The United States are not merely an enlargement of our European culture, still less a mere branch of it; they create a division of that culture into two—themselves and the rest. The line of cleavage does not lie between them and any other sub-group, such as France or England or Italy; it lies between them and *all* Europe.

This first truth, the great division, the separation of the descendant from the original, is our point of departure in all fruitful examination of the problems to which it gives rise. If we underestimate any of the other factors, we go far less wrong than if we under-estimate this. Nor let it be imagined that the truth is any less true because you cannot fix an exact date: a year before

which the things America had in common with
Europe were the more important, and after
which they became the less important. The process or organic change does not allow such pre-
cise boundaries. An oak is most certainly not
an acorn, nor a two-leafed sprout, but you cannot find the moment before which it was not, and
after which it was, an oak. If you take the date
of the Declaration of Independence for your
origin you are at once too late and too early: too
early to admit the effects of new stock, too late
as regards the admission of new ideas. The
effect has been long produced and is now present;
nor can it now possibly be undone; that is the
important thing to seize. Not only a new nation
but a new culture has come rapidly into being.

Next, the rapid and still continuing increase
of the new body in every form has also changed
its international position out of all knowing; so
much so, that the relations between it and
Europe are now, in their immediate and acute
form, directly connected with that increase. The
special political problem which appeared during
the Great War, the question whether America
should or should not join the struggle, was a
direct function of the wealth, the numbers and
the new energies of the United States. The
problems succeeding the Great War in connection with European relations are just as clearly

functions of scale. It is to the vastly superior wealth, the superior man power, and the superior machinery of the New World that conflicting interests of the Old World turn, each for an attempted alliance and for aid.

The succession of various physical stocks is equally remarkable, equally unique in history. There have indeed been many parallels to this in history, parallels in the sense that there have been many examples of population coming in waves to modify an original settlement. But what is peculiar to the growth of the United States is a succession of waves in men *and ideas* alien to and often hostile to the first country of origin, yet immediately forming new and, on the whole, homogeneous material. A culinary metaphor is the nearest. To a small body of original material great additions of quite different ingredients are successively added. Some merge at once, others remain discrete, but the whole composition cooks into something wholly itself and one, and not at all what the first small body was before the process began.

There was early present a considerable negroid element, the like of which was not to be found anywhere in the Old World outside Portugal. The effect of this has profoundly modified the development of society beyond the Atlantic. It was one chief cause in the past of a great civil

conflict. It is the present cause of problems
which the European knows nothing of, which he
cannot visualise, and his ill acquaintance with
which would alone make him misjudge America.

Of our own European stock there came later
a steady and very large Irish immigration, which
was unique in two things: (1) It could be received naturally and easily because it had a facile
medium of communication, it could continue the
original colonial process in language and partly
in blood; and yet (2) it differed violently in religion from the main body of that which received
it. So much was this ease of reception present
that for many years the Irish immigration was
lumped up with all other emigration from the
British Islands. Yet this was also the immigration of families who brought with them a special
antagonism to Britain. You could not have
found, out of all Europe, a source of new immigration more acutely opposed to the spiritual
tradition of that British society from which the
Thirteen Original States had drawn the most of
their blood and institutions.

Then came in successive, though often over-
lapping waves, the North German, the Scandinavian, the Italian and the Slavonic peoples.
Their numbers were not sufficient to divert the
strong direction taken by the new society into
which they poured, but they were amply suffi-

cient to transform its texture; and though an effort has begun to reduce the admixture of these elements, their effect has already taken root. Lately you have had added to this one of those intense organised, sudden Jewish migrations which have played so great a part in all history for two thousand years, and the effect of which on New York in particular and the United States as a whole has already been discussed in these pages.

Such admixture of new stocks in successive arrivals by millions further carries the peculiar mark that *it is in different proportion from the equilibrium of the Old World, social and national;* for (1) the later arrivals have been mainly drawn from the poorer sections of European society, and (2) they have not been drawn in numbers relative to the importance of each culture.

The most striking evidence of this is the anomalous position of the French culture in the United States. It has provided hardly anything of the new immigration, yet the French influence over Europe as a whole has perforce lent to America also a very large element of ideas. You will find the same divergence between ideas and immigrants appearing in regard to the German culture. Here there *has* been a very large numerical addition of German blood. It has un-

doubtedly brought with it certain habits which have merged into the whole body. But the specifically German influence upon American things—much the most notable of which is to be seen in the structure of the universities—did not come from the immigrants, but came through ideas brought in quite apart from the immigrants, and would probably have been present in equal force had there been as little German immigration as there has been French.

In the total resultant of all this, then, you have a society, many members of which can and do claim, not any allegiance to, but a rapidly dwindling affection for certain separate sections of the Old World; an affection which, till quite recently at least, was soon lost in their new surroundings. Yet you also have what is much more important, a general relation between Europe and America which so far forbids indifference and tempts either side to an interference which may yet prove very perilous to both.

If America now attempts to arbitrate in postwar Europe, if one European interest or another captures American support, European and American culture are both doomed to receive wounds which may prove mortal.

The sense of this peril is instinctively expressed upon the American side. It is less apparent on the European, but the latter would be

wise to recognise it more fully than it does. It is perceived more clearly in America than it is in Europe that interference, or as it is called "political entanglement" between the one side of the Atlantic and the other, cannot work smoothly: that any effort so directed will meet with unexpected material and will find itself drawn along unforeseen and distasteful lines. But there is one relation above all where the peril is greatest, where the American instinct of suspicion with regard to it is strongest, and that is the particular relation with England.

It is a most delicate subject to touch. It can hardly be debated without misunderstanding, but it is one upon which clarity is essential if disaster is to be avoided.

The relations between England and the United States are marked by the interplay of two forces, which act independently one of the other, and usually offensively one to the other. We cannot say which of the two is the stronger, for they are of different kinds and incommeasurable. The one is the stream of tradition, institution, language, the other is the profound opposition of the egalitarian to the aristocratic mood. The one force is much more obvious—also more superficial—than the other; but each is present, and each requires definition if we are to understand the nature of the whole matter.

There is no greater distinction between human societies than this distinction between those in which the Equality of Man is an informing religion and those in which the solid organisation of society demands not only a practical inequality but a contempt for the mystical conception of Equality.   Equality has been the rule with civilised men, but by no means the universal rule. The conception that human dignity demands a recognition of human equality is at the basis of all those great states which have seen a civic society as one whole and reduced each of their units to a general standard of subject or citizen under an equal law.   The other idea, the idea that the texture of society demands stratification, the idea that the strength of the State, its very life, can only exist safeguarded by personal, not official, relations of superior and inferior, the idea of privilege as opposed to equal law, the consequent dominance of a class, has informed a much smaller number of societies than the egalitarian idea, but has made those few societies exceedingly strong: these are, historically, the aristocratic societies of the world: that is, the cities and nations in which there was neither king nor popular rule, but the exercise of authority by a revered group of superiors.

There are any number of other cross sections into which you can divide human arrangements;

I have discussed them elsewhere; but for the purpose of the international situation we are now considering this is the distinction: the egalitarian state cannot understand the aristocratic, nor the aristocratic the egalitarian. The one does not merge into the other. The profound ideals of each are alien and incomprehensible and, in acute contact, absurd, one to the other.

Offend Equality in an egalitarian state and you touch a nerve. Men are there provoked by such offence to intense angers. Presume equality in a state of aristocratic tradition and you get no response but laughter.

Now of all states in the modern world the American community is by far the most egalitarian. Not only the doctrine, but the practice of human equality is there more completely accepted, and more actually lived, even than among the Mohammedans of Barbary. The United States belongs historically to the egalitarian group, and stand at the extreme of that group; so that politically and socially they are at one pole of what is, for the purpose of mutual action and aid, a scale of sympathies. The English are at the other.

Of all the modern states the English is still by far the most aristocratic. And though it appears that this aristocratic tradition of England is to-day sinking, it will only so sink at the expense of English strength and greatness. You cannot say that, because the texture of the English community is ceasing to be aristocratic as it once was, therefore it is becoming some new thing, which may be stronger and happier and better than the older England. It is not so. The loss—if indeed we are doomed to it—is the loss of something vital to the English. An Englishman cannot stand indifferent to such a change in the substance of his country, a passionate love of which is the chief source of all he does. One cannot expect such a change of material, in this case, to produce another similar material; any more than one can say of ice, when the day suddenly becomes warmer, that the texture of the ice in becoming more fluid will make a new kind of ice, that the warmth will produce some ice stronger and smoother than the old. When ice melts its very structure and quality disappears.

Historically, England stands among the aristocratic states, and will stand or fall as an aristocratic state. England does not and cannot "democratise" her own structure. Though something of the kind is predicted of her to-day by many observers alien and some few native, it is a false judgment.

For an aristocratic state is not a state in which a class or group has imposed itself by violence. It is not, as men foreign to it perpetually misconceive it to be, a model of injustice. It is a kind of society naturally arranged by the instinct of all its parts, which know, in varying degrees of consciousness, what advantages they derive from the peculiar structure of their commonwealth. The aristocratic states enjoy centuries of domestic order. They have the most continuous and the most successful foreign policy. They have an undying leadership, and so close a union between all their members, so living an identity or personality of the State expressed from the high making and execution of laws and the action of powerful judges, down to the details of education and of domestic life, as makes them live by an intense patriotism. They have, indeed, as I have said on an earlier page, one fatal weakness, which is that they have no machinery of renewal when old age comes upon them. For the populace in them is degraded and cannot act. But that old age comes later than upon their neighbours.

The problem of the relation between England and the United States, therefore, is and will continue to be a problem of two forces at work, wholly different in kind. First, the force that comes from a large community of blood, some community of institutions, and of a far greater community of the most universal medium, which is language. All these unite. But the other

forces, the intimate social and political soul of
each by which the living body of a society is
continued, and which gives that body all its
quality, are not only divergent but exceedingly
antagonistic. That vivid egalitarian spirit in
the American temper is, to the true Englishman,
an intolerable irritant. That which is aristocratic
in the English temper, whether it be acting upwards or downwards, or doing no more than
pursuing one small activity of daily life, is an
intolerable irritant to the American.

To the Englishman the American equality is
an intolerable invasion of his privacy; to the
American the English reserve and silence is an
exasperation. Each is in the eyes of the other
vulgar, insolent, offensive, vain for *exactly* con-
tradictory reasons.

The English public man who "goes down"
(more or less) in the United States is just that
one whom we in England least respect. Whether
the converse is true I do not know.

The contrast here is not only a personal irritant; it ramifies through every social activity and
out into the wide field of international action,
where it becomes a real danger.

The combined effect of these two quite separate sets of forces, the one making for comprehension and sympathy, the other for violent
disunion, cannot be treated as an affair of *plus*

and *minus*. You cannot say: "So much makes for agreement, so much for disagreement, and, on the balance, so much remains on one side or the other." The problem is not of that kind.

If you have relations with a man who is of your own society, education and business, your neighbour, and at the same time devoted to a religion you loathe, you cannot say: "On the whole I am more with him than against him," or the other way about. Your interaction with him will depend upon the function engaged. When the religion is kept in the background, its profound and universal effects on character deliberately checked during mutual intercourse, your town or class or business interests chiefly in play, you are his fellow, and the rest of the world has less in common with you both than you have each with the other. But let a violent public discussion arise turning either directly upon your religion (its persecution and expulsion) or some indirect consequence of your religion, and he is your bitter antagonist. You find in the rest of the world men who are your fellows as against him who becomes your enemy.

If you have relations with a man who is of your own age, but of social manners exasperating to yourself, you will act *and feel* with him in preserving tradition against much younger men who have not the experience to know its necessity.   But in some social quarrel you will act *and feel* with a group of younger men who conform to your standard of manners as against him, supported by another group of younger men who are of his offensive sort.

So it is with these two national currents of which I speak. You cannot say: "On the whole, in a really great crisis, England can depend on America." You cannot say: "Ultimately, in the things that really count, England and America agree." One often hears that sort of talk, especially in England, and it is based on certain truths; but it is valueless because it is off the point, and in its direct statement quite false. You cannot say: "America is so foreign to England and England to America that the more contact you establish the more mutual repulsion you excite." You cannot say: "The United States suspects and will resist British influence beyond any other." There is truth in both statements, but universally applied to policy they are wrong.

I heard a well-travelled Englishman of excellent judgment say (it was during the crisis of the war), "America is very foreign to us, but there is something in her which would forbid her to stand aside if she saw us actually going under." I think he was wrong. It would depend upon the nature of the quarrel which had thus endan-

gered England. If it were a quarrel in which
the *apparent* issue—or that believed to be the
issue by Americans—was of the "law and order"
variety, that is, a war for the preservation of
English power over an alien population, then
England might come to the last straits without
hope of American aid. She would have to depend, as she has depended in the past, upon her
own resources and tenacity, high patriotism, and
aristocratic foreign policy. In her exercise of
all these she is alien to the New World. But if
the struggle were one in which English culture
as part of Western Europe were involved, or
even one involving special English culture on
some point which the United States also accepts
—for instance, the use of commercial opportunities—then the sympathy and in the last resort
the material aid of the United States might appear on the British side.

If Britain could persuade the United States
that some rival, such as France or Italy, was in-
terfering with international commerce wantonly
American opinion would swing strongly to the
British side; but a mere appeal for help on the
plea that we are necessarily, obviously, better
than our rivals, or that the Americans and ourselves are brethren, makes us ridiculous to them
and them contemptuous of us.

To take a concrete example. Suppose a

quarrel, arising over the British position in Egypt, to spread till it became a universal struggle throughout the Old World, and suppose in that struggle the existence of England to be at last imperilled. The support of America would not, I am convinced, depend upon the mere fact that it was England which suffered, any more than if for "England" you should write "France" or "Italy." It would depend upon whether, in American eyes, the war turned on one or other of two issues. If they saw it as an effort to put the Suez Canal under international control, still more as an effort to free the Egyptians from foreign domination, they would oppose us in opinion to the end. If they saw it as an effort to destroy certain institutions which, in name at least, are common to England and America, it would be the other way. Thus, supposing in the struggle the anti-British side to be conducted under a popular continental despotism, while Britain and her allies continued a parliamentary façade of government ("Free Institutions" as they are called), or suppose the issue as a whole to develop into one between Islam and Christendom, with Britain as the champion of Christians, then the opinion of America would appear, I think, on our side, and might, if the danger became grave, support us in arms.

There is no doubt that in this grave point of the relations between England and the United States—a political matter the exact appreciation of reality in which is more important to the English than in any other—a perilous proportion of illusion is admitted upon our side. The English middle class still feels that America is in some way English. It is a vague feeling but a very strong one. It exists in spite of the constant and often exasperating friction aroused by the essential opposition between two exceedingly different kinds of men.

The illusion is even consciously fostered by our upper classes for political purposes. Thus an English Church dignitary recently made the comic remark that "The English and American gentlemen were indistinguishable." He said it with his tongue in his cheek. His motive was patriotic. That illusion is subject to a great deal of modification by experience. But it persists in great strength. Of the English commercial classes the vast majority who have never seen America make the error as a matter of course; even the few who have lived there for some short time come back, as a rule, but half convinced of the truth. The physical differences appal them on the first shock of landing; but they associate as a rule with men of their own level of wealth, see nothing of the people, unconsciously select

impressions according to their more or less remote similarity with the environment at home,
and they will often return with a curious dual
impression which I have heard expressed in such
phrases as: "Unfortunately, ignorant people in
America are brought up on school books which
misrepresent us, but the *best* type of American,"
etc., etc. Or again—more amusing still: "Of
course, the vulgar papers abuse us, but I found
quite a lot of people taking in *The Spectator.*"

There are degrees: an appreciable minority
out of this travelled minority has a strong sensual
memory and a range of vision (or of experience)
beyond the ordinary. These frankly remember
the Americans as foreigners; often liked (with
reservations proper to a foreigner), sometimes
heartily detested; but, anyhow, *foreigners*—
which they most undoubtedly are to us when
they come to Europe and we to them when we
go to America. I have noticed that men thus
accepting reality have a much happier time during their glimpses of the United States than
have their less candid or less intelligent brethren.
It is the man who talks of "Our American
Cousins" that loses his temper when he has to
repeat a phrase three times to be half understood
by an American policeman.

Printed books are a great support of this error.
When an Englishman who has not crossed the

Atlantic sees an American film in London he knows he is looking at something foreign—faces, furniture, social habits, the whole affair. When he sees American caricatures, especially those intended for children—of which there was lately a sudden invasion, now repelled—he is annoyed by their extreme incongruity with what *he* feels about children. But he has read many books from American pens—naturally books suited to the English market, for of most American fiction an Englishman can make nothing. As he read those books they called up innumerable pictures in his mind, for that is the nature of books; and every one of these pictures was a picture of *England*. Had the pictures so formed by his imagination been pictures of France or even Spain he would not have been so vastly misled. But the books being in his own tongue the words "river," "hill," "house," "inn," "tree," and all the rest of the commonest sort stand for English rivers, hills, houses, inns, trees; with now and then a foreign adjunct attached, no doubt, but the article, in the main, just what he has known all his life. Longfellow has some lines on the River Charles which are still familiar to some Englishman. This Englishman who reads them thinks of Trent or Thames. Well, go and see the River Charles! . . . I remember reading as a boy, with responsive enthusiasm, of one (in the Alleghanies perhaps or the Adirondacks) who had inscribed there on a stone: "Thank God for the mountains!" Wales arose in my mind—but when I saw *those* mountains. . . .!

I said at the opening of this book that my reading of American boys' books as a boy had increased the surprise which America gave me. But I think the habit often has another effect, and that modern widely-read men may carry their reading with them as a mask which blurrs their perception of actual things.

If the few English who visit America had none of them read a line of American literature they would get a much sharper and truer impression of that alien universe than they do.

There stands deeply implanted in the English mind *to-day* the conception that political agreement with the United States should be the one unchangeable element in our foreign policy, and that it should be maintained and strengthened at every expense. The conception is as sound as was, till the other day, British dependence on sea power or the fundamental Prussian doctrine that the freedom of Poland would be the death of Prussia. So thoroughly has this principle established itself from the mere force of things, that it has become a part of common patriotism to defend this policy of deference to, and connection with, the United States in every possible way. It is a cardinal maxim of our policy to give way to every American demand, to flatter every American envoy and to applaud every American sentiment in international affairs. The national instinct supports that attitude and will continue to support it as long as America is powerful and united.

This instinct is fully justified. It is as exactly fitted to the modern position of England as has been every popular feeling towards this or that foreign power in the last two hundred years. For during all that time the unerring instinct of the English governing class has served the country as truly as did that of Venice to the preservation and extension of the Common-wealth, and their judgment has informed the whole popular mass of England. Our gentry came to this conclusion upon the due relations with the United States some fifty years ago, and though their former unquestioned leader-ship is now shaken or degraded, some savour of its influence remains.

The policy was deliberate. Until the Civil War the American Republic, distant, compara-tively weak and hostile by tradition, was put upon the list of powers *opposed* to our interests. Its growth alarmed us. The American Civil War was an opportunity for weakening this power, just as the Stuart troubles were an opportunity for Louis XIV. (and that is why he did not whole-heartedly back up James II.), the French civil dissension on religion an opportunity to ourselves and Irish rebellion an opportunity to our enemies.

In no Press throughout Europe was America *then* so heartily reviled as in that of London.

There came at last a moment when Palmerston decided to recognise the South and thus to break up, as he hoped, American unity. Gladstone blurted out the secret at Newcastle: the opportunity was lost.

It may well be that this accident, bitterly regretted at the time in England, was in the long run to her advantage. For the victory of the North, in spite of British aid to the South, or even the reconstruction of the Union (which I am told by good American judges of their own history would have taken place in any case— even if the struggle had ended in a draw) would have left us with an inheritance of permanent and active hostility in the American mind.

As things were, the Union triumphed, a very great power began to grow up rapidly in the New World and the present British policy was founded, the policy of giving way to America in all things, of pretending a natural and seeking a written alliance. Henceforward no provocation whatso-

ever was to outweigh the supreme necessity of
strengthening, from *our* side, every available
connection with the new Great Power. The
Alabama contention was admitted at the beginning of the New Period, the Venezuelan note
swallowed in the middle of it, and only the other
day the debt settlement was made in accordance
with the same unchanging determination. Even
the navy of Britain has been limited without appreciable debate to meet an American demand.
(Though, it is true, on the understanding that it
is to outweigh all the navies of Europe combined.)

Never in modern history was a foreign policy
better justified, more solidly planted, more skil-
fully developed or more tenaciously maintained.
The determination of the British governing class
to purchase American sympathy at *all* costs was
a first-class piece of collective statesmanship,
and has amply justified the superficial humilia-
tions it has involved.

But we have now arrived at a moment when a
question of *method* in the application of that
policy has not only arisen but has become acute.
Is our political connection with the United
States *still* strengthened by the continued sup-
pression of certain truths in the situation, the
continued over-emphasis upon others, which have
been the rule for a generation? I think not. I

think the British relations with America, whatever may have been the case between 1866 and 1914, will henceforward be improved by a recognition of reality and the consequent establishment of a new tone of truth in British political conversation with the United States; it is largely because I feel thus that I have written this book.

I am convinced that too loud cries for help, too crude an appeal in our own behalf as the guardians of international morals, too naïve a reliance upon a supposed American ignorance of all Europe outside England, can only lessen the power of England.

The changed relation of England towards the United States after the great Civil War was naturally supported by the connection of a common language, of many legal institutions with common names (however different in spirit) and of a very real bond between sundry forms of a common Protestant acceptation of history and morals. These were the popular instruments lying ready to hand for those who conducted our Foreign affairs and who framed this section of our foreign policy upon a new model—the very opposite of the old—in the "70's" of the last century, after it had become manifest not only that the Union had conquered but that, on its victory, a vastly increased *power* was to rise beyond the Atlantic.

There went with this new and deliberate policy a mass of propaganda: the putting into currency of certain terms which were suitable to popular use and became commonplaces of English life; adopted to support a national need, but also breeding illusions: "Anglo-Saxon," "English-speaking," and the rest. The public mind on *this* side was encouraged to think in terms of a certain category which included Britain and America, but excluded continental Europe. It readily acceded.

Now had the necessity for the new policy proved a passing one, no great harm would have been done. Aristocratic England has known many such moral comradeships and antagonisms raised for political objects and, at the right moment, diverted or withdrawn. Thus from, say, 1875 to 1904 we had the Russian Tyranny to be abhorred, the German efficiency to be admired; from 1904 to 1918 the German ambition to be first censured and then denounced with frenzy— and so on; from 1918 to the present day the insane and wicked ambition of France is the picture presented. To-morrow it may be the ingratitude of Italy or the shocking success of Poland. This raising artificially of popular moral passion is a most useful and excellent instrument of government so long as the instrument remains supple.

But in the case of the American relation the thing has gone on so long that it has come to seem real—and *therein lies the danger*. Therein lies the danger! England (even educated England) has come to live in an unreal world so far as this particular field of Foreign Policy is concerned, and Foreign Policy is the one political activity in which illusion is fatal.

Every step taken forward on this path weakens England by giving her a scale of values more and more false whereby to judge the forces upon which she relies and those which she has to oppose.

The error branches out into many channels. Thus it is natural for English feeling to work through the connection between a few very wealthy American families and their English acquaintance. To the Americans the association is detestable. In London it looks like a bond. In New York it is an explosive.

Again, we use to Americans certain conventional phrases, giving high moral motives for a piece of financial exploitation in Mesopotamia or Egypt. These phrases have currency among us; we do not take them seriously; we use them as tokens. We proceed to imagine that such phrases have a corresponding currency value in America. It is the greatest possible mistake.

They make us laughed at by many, hated by a few, but supported by no one.

The French have made such errors continually in their foreign relations, putting forward in international debate many a tag of Republican oratory upon Eternal Justice or what not to cover concrete details of policy. We know how such a method fails in their case. We should apply the lesson to our own.

It is similarly an error to treat as typical the friendship of that sort of American whom the Americans call Anglo-Maniac. His emotion is genuine enough, his feeling for England is sincere; but is is hateful to his compatriots.

It is, again, an error to treat a long succession of American diplomatic envoys as though they were mechanical reproductions one of another, to be flattered in exactly the same terms and told in turn that they are each overwhelmingly successful with exactly the same type of success. It is idiotic to sing hymns over those that die. Any American Ambassador at St. James's is a politician who has collared a good post—a political prize. No American regards it as the reward of moral eminence in its captor, and we degrade ourselves in the eyes of all Americans by pretending that it does.

But the worst error of all is the error committed by those who know the truth and who be-

lieve it the part of patriotism to leave their
fellows under misconception. Their motive is
sound. They think that the mirage of an America essentially English will be helpful to their
own country. But their *method* is to-day ill-
chosen. The risks of the modern world have
grown too great and the realities too brutal for
indulgence in illusion.

Mr. Cecil Chesterton, whose knowledge of
the United States was as clear as his love of
England was profound—he gave his life for her
—made it his chief pronouncement that our
cardinal duty *now* in approaching America for
support, sympathy, or even neutrality, was to
approach it as a foreign country. He was a
man who could see reality and had a genius for
describing it. I would that I could acquire
with the profound reverence and affection I bear
to his memory his own crystal lucidity, his in-
comparably exact prose, in which to convince my
every reader of that truth.

*   *   *   *   *

I have spoken thus of the Foreign Relation
of the United States almost entirely in connection
with Great Britain, because the British connection is, as yet, the only one which raises any real
problem. There is for the moment no apparent
peril of American interference in support of

continental Europe, and certainly none of interference by continental Europe with the affairs of America.

There is, on the contrary, a very real peril of disastrous misunderstanding between England and the United States; and that mainly through the completely false picture of the United States presented to the average Englishman, the illusion of an American Commonwealth which is virtually English, and of a world in which the English and the Americans virtually form one body. If this illusion ever be acted upon, catastrophe must come at once; just as catastrophe comes to a man who steps into empty space during a mountain fog under the illusion that he is on solid ground.

If—which the gods avert!—the Government of the United States is brought in to procure some imaginary advantages for England, which the English Government dreads to take of its own strength, then forces will have been let loose in the clash of which the English power over so many subject regions and markets, the English lordship of the sea, will be lost for ever.

Even on the more remote continental connection there is a brief word to be said; it is this: that the incapacity of the one society to understand the other, the utter foreignness of the one society to the other, would lead to unsolvable

problems and unconquerable evils. If at any
moment, through pride, or fanaticism, or cupid-
ity, an attempt were made by the one to order
the affairs of the other neither would succeed and
both would suffer incalculably.

But most of all would England suffer as a
third party. For America would not, as the
simpler politicians imagine, act at England's
orders. She would come in with startlingly independent power.

I have just said that the contingency of an in-
vitation to America by any continental nation
such as France or Italy is now remote; it is
exceedingly improbable that the United States
will be tempted by any continental European
unit to blunder into the complexities of Europe
as a whole, though each European unit would of
course be only too pleased to acquire such an ally
at the expense of the others. The converse, the
interference of the European continent, even
were it consolidated into a confederation of States,
with the affairs of the New World, seems so still
more remote as to be negligible. It is true that
history produces the most surprising contradic-
tions of the most rational guesses, even when
such guesses are made about a near future; but
all my readers will agree, I think, that the probability of a surprise here is very slight. Civil
tumult and disunion among the Americans might

conceivably lead, say, a group in Europe to act in the neighbourhood of the United States, to raid, for instance, the wealth and therefore to control the government of Mexico; but it is hardly conceivable that any such disaster would lead to interference upon the territory of the American Commonwealth itself.

In either case—the improbable, yet possible event, of American arbitration in Europe, the far more improbable event of European interference in America—wisdom must recognise that nothing but disaster could follow from any mixture of two such alien things. There is an instinctive sagacity in the American attitude, so far preserved, of keeping aloof from the affairs of Europe. All those who wish the United States well—and the number of those who wish them well at heart upon our side is small, though the number that flatter them openly is large— all those, I say, who wish the United States well at heart can do no more than repeat the phrase of their great founder, and assure them that the first duty of their rulers is to keep free from all entanglement with the subtleties, the angers, the ultimate conflicts of our own culture.

They saved us in the War. We owe them great debts deliberately undertaken when they were still neutral. Let us pay them, and not whine for assistance.

We of Europe shall solve our own problems; probably by the restoration of the civilised South and West to its proper headship over the rest of the European unity. Things return to their origins, and our Roman unity should revive.

But the process whereby that peace shall be accomplished is not one which could be understood from the standpoint of the United States; it is our own affair; we alone understand it. And let me add this: every public man from Europe, especially every professional politician, who approaches the people of the United States, begging them to interfere in our affairs, is a liar, and knows that he is a liar; his motive for lying is either a desire for self-advertisement and for the limelight (a common motive with politicians) or the nobler motive of patriotism. But be the motive high or low, the inducement offered, the flattering phrases chosen, are lies.

When the power of the United States is thus invoked, it is invoked in order to help one competing European unit against another—France against England, or England against France, bankers against farmers, or farmers against bankers, or what not—and the fine phrases about peace and justice and humanity and civilisation, and the rest of it, are hypocrisy and a poison.

THE END.